Advertising
Account Planning

Advertising
Account Planning
—— A Practical Guide ——

Larry D. Kelley and Donald W. Jugenheimer

M.E.Sharpe
Armonk, New York
London, England

Library of Congress Cataloging-in-Publication Data

Kelley, Larry D., 1955–
 Advertising account planning : a practical guide / by Larry D. Kelley and
Donald W. Jugenheimer.
  p. cm.
 Includes bibliographical references and index.
 ISBN 0-7656-1729-3 (cloth : alk. paper)—ISBN 0-7656-1730-7 (pbk. : alk. paper)
  1. Advertising. 2. Advertising—Management. 3. Advertising campaigns.
 I. Jugenheimer, Donald W. II. Title.

HF5823.K344 2006
659.1′11—dc22   2006003659

Printed in the United States of America

The paper used in this publication meets the minimum requirements of
American National Standard for Information Sciences
Permanence of Paper for Printed Library Materials,
ANSI Z 39.48-1984.

∞

BM (c)   10   9   8   7   6   5   4   3   2   1
BM (p)   10   9   8   7   6   5   4   3   2   1

Contents

Preface and Acknowledgments

Account planning in advertising is a topic and a practice whose time has come. In recent years, account planning has not only become more widely used but in some cases it has evolved into a critical element of advertising campaign planning and execution.

Account planning brings many benefits to the practice of advertising and to the planning and execution of campaigns. Among other things, it:

- Focuses more closely on marketing and advertising goals;
- Relates the goals directly to the strategic and implementation stages of a campaign;
- Coordinates the efforts of the various advertising campaign elements, including research, message, media, production, and traffic;
- Makes the advertising effort more efficient and effective;
- Ascertains that all elements of the campaign are consistent;
- Integrates the marketing, promotion, and selling efforts into the advertising campaign;
- Concentrates on the eventual consumers of the product, service, or idea being marketed;
- Examines the selling process from the perspective of the customers as well as that of the marketers.

Because of its importance in modern advertising, it makes sense to train future practitioners in the arts and practices of account planning, whether that training occurs in formal advertising and marketing courses in colleges and universities, in training programs at advertising companies and agencies, or in a self-taught environment on the job by those who need to use and apply account planning to their work situations. Thus, this book can be used by the students of advertising and marketing, by new employees in the advertising business, and by more experienced advertising practitioners who want to use account planning in their businesses and work.

The book is intended as a practical guide. It is not filled with theories and models and equations. Instead, the book deals with the practical side of account planning: what it is, why it is important, and how to incorporate it into advertising campaign practice and development.

Several other aspects of marketing and advertising are incorporated into the book, including positioning, research, benefit segmentation, creative and message development, media selection, and effectiveness evaluations. Account planning can be utilized throughout the marketing process and the book shows how this is done and how to make it work.

In addition, there are three practical in-depth cases from the real practice of advertising: one on a packaged-good marketing situation, one on retail advertising, and one on business-to-business advertising.

Throughout the book, there are helpful elements at the end of each chapter. These aids include questions to help the reader review and understand what was in the chapter, possible discussion topics to further the analysis of account planning information, a practical case that can be followed throughout the book from one chapter to another to apply the chapter knowledge to a real-world situation, and sources for finding additional information on each topic.

The book has been written by two experienced authors of widely used advertising materials: one is an advertising agency executive with many years of account planning experience and the other is an advertising professor who has taught thousands of college students how to appreciate, use, and benefit from advertising. Together, these two backgrounds and strengths have come together to provide a unified learning experience.

Use the book as it was intended: as a teaching and learning aid as well as a resource for those who actually practice the art and science of account planning in advertising.

The authors thank the following people for their help and support during the writing and editing of this book: Kyle Allen, Ken Bielicki, Melanie Ford-Weir, and Steve Smith of FogartyKleinMonroe, who provided information, examples, and insights that greatly enhanced the book. The authors would especially like to thank Debbie Thompson, who worked hard to make the book appear in its final form. Her dedication and abilities to coordinate, understand, and interpret have been invaluable and her contributions have made for a better book. Finally, the authors thank their spouses and families for their support, without which this project could not have been possible.

Advertising
Account Planning

Chapter 1

What Is Account Planning?

Every member of a company is responsible for its success by enhancing its brand equity. Perhaps you are a brand manager responsible for a specific brand or portfolio of brands. Maybe you are the president of a company or a marketing director. Or maybe you are an account planner, or account manager, or even president of an advertising agency. Perhaps you are in charge of developing a hypothetical advertising campaign for an advertising or marketing class. Regardless of your title or situation, how your brand or company is positioned and perceived in the marketplace is crucial to your success.

Positioning your brand and then figuring out how that positioning is to be reflected in all forms of communications can be a daunting task. Ensuring that all the time you spend positioning the brand is properly executed internally within the company and externally among the consumers is vital to the growth of the brand. There is nothing more disturbing to a brand manager than when the sales force sells the brand as an inexpensive alternative to another brand while the agency is advertising it as a premium product. Or perhaps you have positioned the brand to appeal to a discriminating adult only to find that your media plan is targeting the great unwashed. Yet these types of disconnects happen every day in hundreds of companies.

It can be a difficult task to pull together a brand's position and to get that position properly reflected in all the appropriate marketing communications in the marketplace. The process itself can be confusing and sometimes elusive. The simple fact is, you cannot develop relevant communications and then hope to evaluate its impact on the brand without proper planning. The purpose of this book is to help bring clarity to the job of linking brand positions and communications. This task revolves around the art and science of account planning.

Account planning can be a job or a department, or it might be a process within an advertising agency or within a marketing group. No matter how account planning is being handled on your brand, it is one of the most important aspects of getting your brand ready for the growth it deserves.

Origins of Account Planning

To understand the origins of account planning requires a bit of a history lesson in advertising, along with an understanding of consumer behavior. Although the history of account planning has its origins in the United Kingdom, the reason for the rise and adoption of account planning is truly an international tale.

In the 1950s, advertising agencies were still the main pioneers of marketing research. At the time, advertising agencies had large market research staffs or subsidiaries that conducted all sorts of marketing analyses and compiled information on consumer behavior trends and research. At that time, advertising agencies served in the role of strong consultants to clients on all aspects of marketing and communications.

This situation began to change in the 1960s when consumer products companies were restructured along marketing lines. This era was the beginning of the brand management approach used by many companies today. During this period of transition, the relationship between client and advertising agency changed as well. The clients, with their brand managers, brought market research into the company so that they could devise their own research programs. This shift put advertising agencies in more of a specialist role, working on communications only. As a result, research was more and more isolated from the advertising agency process and product. Consumer understanding and knowledge was yanked away from the advertising agencies, which were struggling to cope with this change.

In the late 1960s, two UK advertising agencies, Boase Massimi Pollitt (BMP) and J. Walter Thompson of London (JWT), started what is today called account planning. Each agency came to advertising account planning from a different direction. Boase Massimi Pollitt developed an enhanced role for the researcher, who up until that time had typically been a "backroom" specialist. The BMP model put this research person alongside the account management and creative personnel as an equal in planning and directing the advertising for a client's business. At about the same time, JWT merged its marketing department with its media and research departments and called it "account planning." Both agencies made their respective changes in an effort to gain a closer look at consumer situations and problems and at subsequent creative solutions.

Advertising account planning, as we know it, began to take shape in the United Kingdom in the 1970s. Account planning groups were formed in the late 1970s to bring together a discipline that had various roots, practices, and criteria. It was highlighted in 1979 when England's Account Planning Association shifted its advertising International Planning Awards from creative pretesting of advertisements to the use of planning and strategy as a gauge for advertising effectiveness. This shift also set the stage for some account planners to break away and form their own advertising agencies. Clients quickly followed suit and supported this new type of planning-discipline agency.

Account planning was subsequently introduced to New York by Jay Chiat of the Chiat/Day advertising agency in the late 1980s, because he felt that more innovative and compelling advertising was coming out of the United Kingdom rather than from the United States. The people at Chiat/Day were very successful in importing a UK planner to aid in their creative rise, which included introduction of the famous 1984 Macintosh computer commercial along with other noted advertising campaigns. Chiat/Day's success led other U.S. advertising agencies to bring in account planning people, largely from the United Kingdom, to their shops. One such planner was Jon Steel, who migrated to Goodby, Silverstein and Partners in the late 1980s. His 1998 book *Truth, Lies, and Advertising: The Art of Account Planning* was the tipping point for the recognition and adoption of account planning into the mainstream of many advertising agencies across the United States.

As late as the mid-1980s, there was no account planning function within advertising agencies in the United States. Now the American Association of Advertising Agencies (4As) holds an annual conference for account planning, attracting hundreds of account planners and many others who want to learn more about this relatively new discipline within the advertising agency community.

Changing the Fundamentals

The origins of advertising account planning rest with two advertising agencies that saw the need for someone to bridge the gap between the traditional research function and the account management function within the agency. It was an elevated role for research but filled by people who were better at interpreting research in a usable, pragmatic manner, rather than by technical researchers. Over time, account planning has come to be recognized as a way to make advertising more effective by early integration of consumers and their attitudes into the advertising development process.

For many agencies, advertising account planning has become the fourth pillar of agency functions, along with creative, media, and account management. Those who have adopted account planning see it as a different skill set, separate from account management or research, but one that spans both areas. Traditionally, account executives are busy tending to client needs while researchers often are primarily concerned with research techniques and quantitative methods. The account planner fills the gap or void in this process by synthesizing consumer information that must be thoroughly considered in the creation and evaluation of advertising.

This fundamental change, inserting an account planner into the process as an equal to account management and creative work groups, has had a profound effect on each area. For the account managers, it meant giving up some control of the advertising strategy process to another person; for the creative group, it meant that message development would be influenced during the development process by a consumer advocate. This fundamental shift is why advertising account planning has had its share of skeptics and development problems within the agency community.

What Does an Account Planner Do?

In its purest form, the role of the advertising account planner is part of the advertising creative process. The product of the account planner is typically in the form of a creative brief, which forms the basis from which the creative group executes various forms of advertising message content.

However, in its broadest context, the account planner is the representative of the consumer in question. The advertising account planner's role is to understand the consumer, much like an actor understands his character in a play. By truly immersing themselves in the consumer, the account planners can add value to a wide variety of both advertising and business areas.

While advertising account planners certainly know a lot about research and use research in their function, they are not traditional market researchers. A researcher finds out about the consumer; a good account planner identifies with the consumer and internalizes the consumer. A researcher may paint a picture of the consumers; an account planner should be able to tell not only who the consumers are but also what they feel. It is a state of mind that separates an account planner from a pure researcher.

From an advertising point of view, the account planner should be inserting the consumer's viewpoint all along the path of creating advertising, rather than serving as a researcher testing ideas after the creative work has been completed. This is one of the fundamental reasons why account planning took hold in the United Kingdom and continues to gain traction in the United States. The

Figure 1.1   **The Client Is at the Center of the Advertising Process**

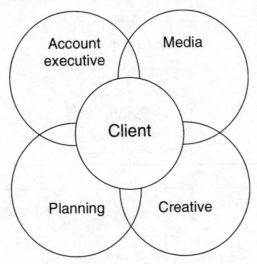

account planning process engages the consumers in their emotional reactions to advertising, rather than a more rationale creative testing being used to determine creative success or failure. This change is not meant to denigrate the role of the researcher; it is merely a different way of implementing the process of creative advertising. Figure 1.1 shows how the client (the advertiser) is central to the process of advertising planning and creativity.

Depending on the organization, an account planner can be an advertising strategist, a business consultant, a consumer ombudsman for creative and/or media activity, or just a producer of creative briefing documents. It all depends upon the talents of the people and the commitment the organization may or may not have to advertising account planning. Figure 1.2 shows how the advertising agency may be organized.

Impact of Account Planning

Account planning is the one area that can link all the elements of brand communication with the positioning of the brand itself. As the consumer advocate, the advertising account planner is involved in every facet of the brand's strategy and its reflection in marketing communications.

Perhaps the most important decision made in marketing a brand or service is how it will be positioned and how believable and unique that positioning is with the consumer. Brand positioning plays a critical role in the

Figure 1.2   **Typical Advertising Agency Organization**

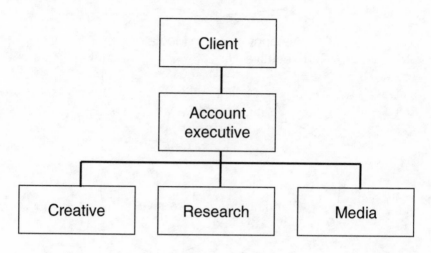

success or failure of the marketing program for that brand. The balancing act for effective brand positioning is to match a business objective with how consumers view the brand.

Advertising account planning must help facilitate the brand positioning process. Often, the greatest conflict within an organization is how the company views the brand compared to how consumers view the brand. Ultimately, how consumers view your brand is the key to having your brand's position validated in the marketplace. For example, in the early 1980s, NCR came out with an advertising campaign that said, "NCR means computers." Consumers replied that NCR means National Cash Register, and cash registers are not computers. NCR never recovered from this positioning blunder and promptly went out of the computer business.

So positioning is not only what your brand is but it is also a statement of what your brand is not. In this case, NCR had a business or marketing objective of being in the computer business. However, the company grossly misjudged its consumer equity, which placed NCR in the older cash register or business machine category. As a result, the marketing objective and the brand were at a disconnect. Had NCR simply said that it was a leader in business machines with the computer being just a more sophisticated machine, perhaps the consumers would have been more willing to accept the proposition. The point is that positioning is the essence of the brand. Solid account planning can help marketers to arrive at this brand essence.

Account Planning Links Advertising Strategy with Positioning

Getting past the positioning hurdle can take several months of work. Sometimes it is a tedious process to get to the essence of the brand. As quickly as you can say "30-second commercial," all that hard work and careful crafting of a brand position can be for naught if your advertising strategy does not link up with the brand's position.

The role of advertising account planning is to assist in linking that positioning strategy to advertising strategy and to help lead the creative charge to convey the brand's position properly and clearly. It all seems so logical. Yet it is often in the creative process that things can go terribly awry.

Advertising agencies are evaluated largely on how their creative product works. Sometimes the charge is to make that "breakthrough commercial" that wins Clio Awards and gets the advertiser a lot of attention. In an effort to develop these memorable commercials, agencies and their advertisers can lose sight of the brand's positioning.

For example, the Subway sandwich chain has staked out a position as a healthy alternative to the other fast-food "burger" fare. The Subway spokesman, Jared, lost many pounds eating Subway sandwiches and is a great demonstration for that healthy-food positioning. Along the way, the advertising took a "creative" turn with a "sock puppet" as a new mascot to sing the praises to fresh sandwiches. One flight of television advertising was enough to convince Subway that the "sock puppet" wasn't the answer. Today, Jared is still the icon of Subway and continues to do a solid job in communicating Subway's value proposition.

Translating the positioning strategy into advertising strategy and creative executions of that strategy is vitally important to the brand. Advertising account planning is the link that brings it all together.

Media Support Brand Positioning

There is no way positioning will be successful if it is not adequately and accurately supported through the advertising media selection and placement. If you want the positioning to be successful, you must select media that are effective, efficient and, above all, accurately reflect the positioning.

In fact, the media selection itself can be an aspect of how the positioning is reflected. For example, Absolut vodka has carved out a fantastic brand position and the creative message is executed brilliantly. One of the key decisions the clients made was always to have their advertisements on the back cover of the magazines in which they advertised. Over time, the back cover became as big a part of the brand's being as the creative message itself.

As media choices become increasingly fragmented, there is a real opportunity to align brand strategy with media selection. If your brand is positioned for "rugged individualists," then the media planners should select appropriate media vehicles. Scheduling a commercial on the Lifetime cable network, or on a soft-rock station, or in *Good Housekeeping* magazine might not be in keeping with that positioning. Rather, one might select boating or motorcycling magazines or outdoor programs to carry the advertising campaign.

The trend today is for advertising account planning to play a role in the media aspect of the advertising campaign. With all the complexities of the media world, it is not only appropriate but also critical for the advertising account planner to view the media plan with an eye toward brand-positioning synergies.

Why Should I Care About Account Planning?

So, what is the big deal about advertising account planning? Advertising has always been planned and campaigns have always been measured in some manner. Advertising luminaries such as Claude Hopkins, Rosser Reeves, David Ogilvy, Leo Burnett, and Bill Bernbach were all superb planners. So, aren't we doing this already? Do we really need a separate department or function for this activity? Isn't the advertising account planner really just a glorified qualitative researcher? What is the return on investment (ROI) for the account planner?

All are valid questions and have been debated internally and externally within the advertising agency community, both in the United States and abroad. The rise of the information age has greatly increased the need for account planning within the advertising agency. The reason for this is simple. As consumer information became more prevalent and reliable, advertisers and marketers took control of the consumer away from the advertising agency community. At one time, marketers looked primarily to their advertising agencies for consumer insights and acumen. Now, they often look to the advertising agency solely for creative execution of their own insights.

However, it can be dangerous to confuse pure information with true consumer insight. Just because you can count every raindrop doesn't mean you are smart enough to get out of the rain. This is where the advertising account planner comes in. He or she is the interpreter of this vast reservoir of information that can result in pinpointed, poignant marketing communications.

Another reason why account planning is so valuable in the United States is because of the marketplace itself. With a maturing marketplace for many goods and services in the United States, it is very difficult to differentiate one's brand on some sort of unique attribute. This maturation means that the differentiation is more likely to be based on an emotional benefit rather than on a rational one. Helping guide marketers through the emotional maze is a cornerstone of an account planner's job.

So for the advertising community, the account planner is one of the keys to swinging the pendulum back in favor of agencies as the entities who offer consumer insights. They are the ones who are leading the charge to add humanity to the reams of information about customers and to help marketers tap into the emotional needs of those consumers with relevant and compelling advertising. One can certainly make the case that account planning is a new spin on ideas fostered by the advertising luminaries previously listed. As David Ogilvy once said, "You don't stand a tinker's chance of producing successful advertising unless you start doing your homework." Frankly, that is largely what advertising account planning is all about. It is doing the homework that leads to compelling content through an engaging contact plan.

Advertising account planning can be a job, a process, or a way of approaching business. Regardless of what it is in the organization, it should become the mindset for all those involved in the campaign. Advertising account planning is keeping the consumer at the center of the marketing and advertising universe. That is why we should care about the principles of account planning.

Review Questions

1. How does advertising account planning differ from research?
2. How does account planning differ from account management?
3. How does account planning bring the various marketing and advertising functions together?
4. In account planning, what is the role of the advertising agency? How does it differ from the agency's broader role in the general practice of advertising?

Discussion Questions

1. Why would research be quantitative while account planning is qualitative? What is meant by "qualitative"? Give some examples.

2. How can account planning work effectively with so many different advertising functions?
3. Why does account planning function at all levels of the marketing and advertising effort, rather than at one level?
4. How does the job description of the account planner differ from that of the account supervisor or account executive?

Exercises

Go to a large grocery store. Look at the array of items for sale within each product category, for example, laundry detergents. Try to discern the differences between the products within a single category: in effectiveness claims, packaging, form (liquid vs. powdered detergents, for example), usage instructions, package sizes, extensions of product lines, and position on store shelves. How might account planning work for each of these product differences?

CBC Case Study

The Carbonated Beverage Company (CBC) is a small, regional manufacturer and bottler of soft drinks. It is known in the industry for being a cagey marketer and tough competitor. The company is known among its customers for its fresh, zingy flavors of soda. However, the company must work very hard to compete with the larger and better-known companies that produce and sell soft drinks, such as Coca-Cola and Pepsi.

Concentrate on the following analyses of the market situation for CBC.

1. What are possible features that could be used in promoting CBC's products?
2. What possible market niches or specialized areas are there for CBC?
3. What are the existing disadvantages for CBC in the marketplace?
4. What possible advantages exist for CBC?
5. So far, this case has used two names for this product category: soft drinks and soda. How many other names for this product category exist in the United States? How many exist in the English language? To what extent are these various names linked with particular regions of the country? Why are there so many different product-category names for this product?
6. Go to a large grocery store and look at the array of carbonated soft drinks for sale. Why are there so many different brands and flavors? What other differences are there between various soft drinks offered for sale? Who might purchase each type of soft drink?

Additional Sources

Hackley, Christopher. "Account Planning: Current Agency Perspectives on an Advertising Enigma." *Journal of Advertising Research* 43, no. 2 (June 2003): 235–45.

Kessler, Stephen. *Chiat/Day.* New York: Rizzoli, 1990.

Ries, Al, and Jack Trout. *Positioning: The Battle for Your Mind.* New York: McGraw-Hill, 2001.

Samuel, Larry. *The Trend Commandments: Turning Cultural Fluency into Marketing Opportunity.* New York: Bang! Zoom! Books, 2003.

Stabiner, Karen. *Inventing Desire. Inside Chiat/Day: The Hottest Shop, the Coolest Players, the Big Business of Advertising.* New York: Simon & Schuster, 1993.

Steel, Jon. *Truth, Lies, and Advertising: The Art of Account Planning.* New York: Wiley, 1998.

Chapter 2
Situation Analysis

Just as you would not have a physician treat you without first providing a thorough diagnosis, you cannot make an advertising recommendation to a company without first understanding the company's complete situation. Just as in the case of the doctor—who must understand the skeleton, the central nervous system, and the arterial system—your diagnosis of any company is multifaceted.

In reviewing a company's situation, you should review the company from a business, a brand, a consumer, and a communications perspective. Any review should assess both external as well as internal forces that may impact the company.

As an advertising account planner, you will want to balance business realities with perceptual realities of the consumer marketplace. This is where your analysis is typically broader than that of a standard business consultant, who may review the firm from only one business perspective, such as finance or management, but not from a consumer or brand viewpoint.

SWOT Analysis

The traditional business analysis that most companies use to assess their market position and that of their competitors is called SWOT analysis. SWOT stands for:

- Strengths
- Weaknesses
- Opportunities, and
- Threats.

Strengths and weaknesses are typically internal assessments about the company itself, while opportunities and threats are looking at outside influences that may affect the company's position and future.

Figure 2.1 **Wheel of Competitive Strategy**

Strengths and Weaknesses

The fundamental question you have to ask yourself is, "How and why are we better than our competitors?" Conversely, "How and why are we worse than our competitors?" These are not always easy questions to answer honestly. As an advertising account planner, your role is to be an objective third party to facilitate honest dialogue about the company and how it can capitalize on its strengths and shore up to overcome its weaknesses.

Figure 2.1 shows a strategic wheel that is helpful in guiding a company through this analytical process. As you can see, there is a blend of hard business factors—such as financial strength, market share, and product quality—along with more perceptual factors—such as brand equity and communications strength of the advertising. It is important to look at each side of the equation to help the company gain insight into how best to grow its business. After you conduct this analysis on the company, it is equally important to look at the immediate competitors to determine their strengths and weaknesses. This internal evaluation and comparison against your competitors sets the stage for looking at the opportunities.

Opportunities

In assessing the opportunities of the company, keep in mind that markets are dynamic and that new opportunities continually evolve. You may want to set up criteria for short-term and longer-term opportunities. You may also want to look at trends that are competitive in nature and those trends that are consumer-oriented.

For example, from your strength and weakness assessment, you may have discovered that your competitor is retrenching and is pulling out of a market. This would signal a short-term opportunity to increase your share by filling that void. This is a great example of a short-term opportunity driven by competition.

But not all opportunities are as easy to see as this one. There are two layers of opportunities that you will want to identify for a company. The first layer is the obvious opportunities, such as going after new geographic or target market segments or adding more product features to the portfolio. The second layer of trends comes from understanding where consumer trends are headed and capitalizing on them.

For example, there is currently a trend among consumers to be watchful about consuming calories. If you were a food manufacturer, this might lead you to develop a low-cal strategy in terms of new products and/or marketing communications. This analysis could lead to segmenting your audience differently than in the past. If your product fits in with this trend, you might use it as a tool to increase your price.

Trends as Opportunities

As an account planner, one of your central roles is to help clients understand what trends are emerging and how to capitalize on them. While that sounds like a noble mission, how do analysts actually spot trends?

There are a couple of paths that may be followed in seeking out trends. The first path is to subscribe to trend research. The leading research firm in the field of trends is Yankelovich Partners, Inc. The Yankelovich firm has been studying the American consumer since 1971. The Yankelovich Monitor is conducted on an annual basis, serving many companies with a look into consumer attitudes, values, and lifestyles. Each year, Yankelovich conducts in-person, door-to-door interviews with 2,500 adults over age 16. This interview, coupled with a self-administered, leave-behind questionnaire, forms the basis for the firm's ongoing tracking study that has been a mainstay in analyzing American culture for decades.

There are many other research companies that are focused on consumption trends. One such resource is Iconoculture, a strategic consumer advisory services company offering a unique method of evaluating trends within the context of consumer values. Rather than fielding an ongoing study as

Yankelovich does, Iconoculture relies on a strategic team of research analysts who constantly feed observations and trends to a large database, and consumer strategists who analyze them for their underlying consumer values. These identified trends are then plotted against 136 consumer values and rolled up into a set of forty-three macrotrends.

For example, one of the forty-three macrotrends Iconoculture identifies is called "Ready, Set, Go!^{SM}" This macrotrend is the combination of innovation plus convenience. A great example of applying this analysis is Home Depot's plan to test convenience stores in its parking lots. For companies that want to reach "baby boomers," this macrotrend is an important ingredient to marketing to this group. The whole notion of convenience, access, and time efficiency is a cornerstone of "baby boomer" values that are reflected in this trend. Understanding these types of trends can lead to new and better marketing as well as more efficient and more economical marketing communications (see Figure 2.2).

There are many other specific trend companies that focus on a specific market group such as children or on a specific industry such as food. All of these companies are great at offering you the basic building blocks to understanding what trends might be emerging in society and how those changes might impact your client's brand.

Finally, you may want to conduct your own primary research among consumers. Motivational research techniques and ethnographic research are methods whereby researchers get at the deeper meanings that underlie a brand in consumers' opinions. This type of research, conducted over time, can help spot shifts in attitudes that can ultimately impact the client's brand or company.

Threats

If you are the brand manager of Tide laundry detergent and Clorox decides to launch a new laundry detergent brand that cleans twice as well as your brand, there is little doubt that it's a threat to your brand's existence.

Immediate threats like this are readily apparent. If you are on your toes, a move like this shouldn't come as a surprise to you. Threats can come from a variety of directions, so you should expand your thinking to go beyond the standard competitive set when thinking about a competitive threat. It is often said your strengths are sometimes your greatest weaknesses. In looking at threats, it is a good idea to evaluate areas that may look like a positive but may backfire to cause you danger or harm.

For example, if you are a number three brand in your product category,

Figure 2.2

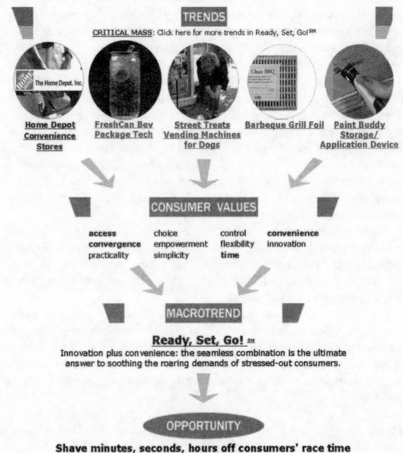

Source: Iconoculture 2004. Reprinted with permission.

the distribution channel currently carrying your brand may turn out to be a larger threat than your "competitor." With the current rapid consolidation in the retail arena, private label brands from a Kroger in the grocery arena or Home Depot in the home improvement market may be more of a threat to your existing shelf space than is the danger from any single manufacturer. So the strength of being stocked and promoted by a major retailer may turn to a threat if that retailer wants to market the same item that you manufacture.

In today's rapidly changing world, an online channel may change the dynamic balance of the marketplace and you could wind up on the outside looking in.

Competition can come either from a like competitor or from a distribution channel. Another threat could come from how you make your product. If you are a coffee brand and there is a shortage of coffee beans, the tight inventory is a threat even to the basic task of putting the brand on the shelf or to selling your product at a price that consumers can afford. A chain of family-oriented motels might think that its greatest threat comes from other hotel chains when the real threat is the rapidly rising cost of gasoline, which may discourage family travel.

The most obvious threats are typically readily identified. Most companies have intelligence regarding their competition, distribution channels, and supply of raw materials. Even in a service business—such as airlines, shipping, retailing, or tax preparation—identifying competitive threats and potential cost issues are a matter of normal business intelligence gathering.

What separates the good brands from the great brands is identifying consumer trends that might be a threat to the business. For example, in early 2002, there were the beginnings of a trend toward eating fewer carbohydrates as a method to lose weight. This was started some twenty years before with the Atkins diet, but in 2002 the trend began to catch hold and become more mainstream. The South Beach diet, a friendlier Atkins-type diet, came into vogue and soon stalwarts such as Weight Watchers and others were following suit. The potato, rice, and pasta industries were slow to respond and took a severe hit in short-term sales. Interestingly, this low-carb craze was a part of a larger trend identified by Iconoculture as "Wellville.[SM]" Wellville seeks total well-being through the balance of self, community, and world. Although this may sound a bit inflated and self-important, the notion of balance has been a populist mantra among the baby boom generation. It played itself out in the low-carb craze where popular sentiment rallied against the "no carb" crowd to say that a certain amount of carbs is good and there are "good and bad carbs," much like there is good and bad cholesterol. The moral of this story is: had the potato, rice, and pasta groups followed this larger macrotrend and just fit into the overarching consumer trend, they would not have been as weakened as they were by fighting against the carb counters.

The SWOT analysis is a great tool for discussion and prioritization of the opportunities that the brand has today and in the future. The action plans that come out of a SWOT analysis should include a short-term goal to stem any immediate threats or capitalize on any immediate opportunities.

The second action plan should be a longer-range plan that builds on the brand's strengths while working to shore up against any glaring weaknesses. All of these future plans are worthless without a customer perspective that can truly add the most value to this exercise.

Organizational Storytelling

The SWOT analysis is predominantly a left-brain exercise. It is an assessment and is clinical in nature. While you can add some dimension to this exercise in the form of consumer knowledge, it is still largely an analytical exercise.

To balance out the SWOT analysis with something more right-brain in nature, you may want to embark upon drafting an organization narrative or story. Storytelling is becoming a more widely accepted method of helping management and marketing better understand their own company or brand in terms that anyone can comprehend.

The storyteller develops a story much in the same way a company develops a SWOT analysis. However, unlike the SWOT analysis, most stories are highly engaging. This is why innovative companies, such as 3M, are moving to storytelling as a means of business planning. The more engaging the plan, the better chance it will have of taking root in the organization.

The first order of business for the storyteller is to determine what the protagonist wants or desires. Desire is the essential lifeblood of any story. In the case of business, the desire is the corporate or brand goal. Is it to be the very best or simply known as the best, or to move into new markets, or to quash a competitor? Obviously, to paint a picture of the company or of a brand, you must know its strengths, the "S" in the SWOT, plus its values and personality.

The point of storytelling is to put a human face on what is a basically a relatively clinical exercise. The greatest benefit of storytelling is that human beings naturally want to work through stories. Stories are how we remember things, rather than by using to-do lists or the endless sea of Power Point presentations that are foisted on corporate America. "What is your story?" is a common question that you might ask of someone new whom you are meeting for the first time. The same is true in business.

Making the company the protagonist of the story, or the central character with brand or corporate strengths as value statements, is the beginning of how a SWOT analysis becomes a story. In his quest to seek the opportunity, the hero must overcome his weaknesses and slay outside threats.

Figure 2.3   **Hansel and Gretel as SWOT Analysis**

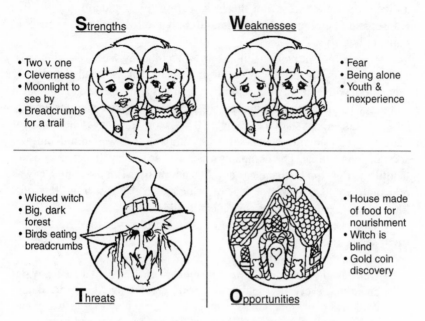

Strengths

- Two v. one
- Cleverness
- Moonlight to see by
- Breadcrumbs for a trail

Weaknesses

- Fear
- Being alone
- Youth & inexperience

- Wicked witch
- Big, dark forest
- Birds eating breadcrumbs

- House made of food for nourishment
- Witch is blind
- Gold coin discovery

Threats

Opportunities

Let's go through the steps of the story. The first order of business for the storyteller is to determine what the protagonist wants or desires. In the case of business, the desire is the goal or opportunity. To tell a story or to paint a picture of the company, you must know its strengths. These attributes will become the basis of the company's values and personality.

The desires themselves may be the opportunities that you have outlined in the SWOT analysis. But you must first slay those angry dragons of weakness and get to those rewarding opportunities.

Once you have the basis for the story, your next job is to decide how your protagonist should act to achieve these desires in the face of such antagonistic forces. It is in the answer to that question that storytellers reveal the truth about their characters, for most characters are revealed in the choices they make in their lives.

Let's reverse the process a bit and tell the story of Hansel and Gretel as a SWOT analysis (see Figure 2.3). Everyone knows the story of Hansel and Gretel and the evil witch. Hansel and Gretel had some character strengths, such as being clever and innovative, which led them to leave a breadcrumb trail so they wouldn't get lost in the forest. They also had to overcome some weaknesses and fears. The evil witch was a major threat, as were the dark forest and the birds eating the breadcrumb trail. But Hansel and Gretel prevailed and got not only the food but also some gold coins to boot.

Now let's look at how to tell a story of a company. The following is an example of a brief story for Waste Management. This company had a poor reputation, with a history of accounting scandals and past associations with gangsters in the trash-hauling business. However, under new leadership, Waste Management started to reinvent itself, from a garbage-hauling company to a vast environmental-services company that was introducing all sorts of innovations. The company was a leader in recycling and in using landfills to develop methane gas as a fuel alternative. But the company was reluctant to tell its story for fear of bringing up the past transgressions. Plus, it was unsure whether customers would really care about the firm's story. However, through a series of events, the story was told. Here is one small segment of it.

> One day, the leader of the world's greatest environmental company decided that everyone should know what great things they were doing. Although many told him to be quiet, he just could not for he was proud of his associates' accomplishments. So, he rang bells and handed out advertisements that told of the wondrous things the company was doing to help its customers and the earth. And the people were amazed and rejoiced. They had no idea that great things had been going on for so long. Not only did they think *better of the company, they also paid handsomely for its services.*

Your story can be a summary or it can be a very long story that chronicles specific events and details specific strengths, weaknesses, threats, and opportunities. It is largely up to you. The point of the storytelling exercise is to dramatize the outcome the company is trying to achieve and to put a more human face on what can be a rather dry exercise.

Both SWOT analysis and storytelling can be important tools for the advertising account planner, and both of these tools can be used in concert with one another.

Review Questions

1. How do brands gain shelf space in retail stores?
2. What blocks some brands from gaining shelf space?
3. What is "brand equity"? How can a company gain brand equity?

4. What are the disadvantages of a company's having a limited promotion budget in facing its competition? How might a company work to overcome such a disadvantage?
5. How is storytelling different from SWOT analysis?

Discussion Questions

1. Why do people buy and consume certain products, such as chocolate candy or soft drinks?
2. Why do people buy and consume certain brands of those products?
3. What benefits do people gain from consuming such products?
4. What benefits do people gain from consuming certain brands of those products?
5. How can storytelling uncover a firm's or a brand's strengths or weaknesses that might not be discovered through the use of SWOT analysis?

Exercises

Analyze the basic products of the largest brands of toothpaste: Crest, Colgate, Close-Up, and others. How do they differ from one another and from other competitors?

How much of that differentiation is in the products themselves and how much is because of promotion factors? How can toothpaste brand sales be increased through product line extension? Tell the story of Crest toothpaste and how it has fared in the marketplace.

CBC Case Study

Go back and review the CBC case from Chapter 1, along with your responses to the assigned questions for that chapter. Use that information to provide the information below.

1. How and why is CBC better than its major competitors?
2. How and why is CBC worse than its major competitors?
3. Analyze CBC's product and position from various perspectives: the owners of the firm; the consumers of the firm's products; the brand manager; the communications, such as advertising; the substitutability for the product; the brand equity; the consumer and market trends.
4. Convert your analysis to a SWOT analysis for CBC.
5. Now tell the story of CBC using a fairytale as your model.

Additional Sources

Allan, Julie, Gerard Fairtlough, and Barbara Heinzen. *The Power of the Tale: Using Narratives for Organizational Success*. New York: Wiley, 2002.

Hollensen, Svend. *Global Marketing: A Decision-Oriented Approach*. London: Prentice, 2004.

Morgan, Adam. *Eating the Big Fish: How Challenger Brands Can Compete Against Brand Leaders*. New York: Wiley, 1999.

Neuhauser, Peg. *Corporate Legends and Lore: The Power of Storytelling as a Management Tool*. New York: McGraw-Hill, 1993.

Rackham, Neil. *Spin Selling*. New York: McGraw-Hill, 1988.

Samuel, Larry. *Passion Points: Turning Consumer Passion into Marketing Opportunity*. New York: Bang! Zoom! Books, 2004.

Chapter 3

Understanding the Customer

The fundamentals of developing a business proposition require you to understand the customers and respond to their needs. These requirements seem so basic, yet many marketers and business leaders really don't fully understand what makes their customers tick.

As an account planner, putting yourself in the customer's shoes and then being able to communicate this learning to help drive both business and communications strategy is the most important part of your job. You should know both the facts and the figures about the customers as well as what motivates them to purchase your client's brand.

This chapter is a high-level view of what is required to understand the customer. There are many texts offering a much more detailed and in-depth view of consumer behavior. Here, we will not be going into a large-scale discussion of motivational research techniques and analysis. However, we will offer a fundamental look at how you go about understanding the customer, forming the foundation for the next chapter, which is devoted to defining the target market.

Who Is Buying My Brand?

The most basic start to understanding the customer begins with the question, "Who is buying my brand or service?" If you are a consumer-goods manufacturer, you might have millions of consumers buying your product. If you are marketing turbine engines, you may only have a handful of customers or prospects. Regardless of the number, the place to begin is with a count of customers.

It is important to know how many people are buying your product and what percentage of the population they make up. By understanding the penetration level both for your brand and for the category in which you compete, you can see what the high-water mark currently is in the category. This is a key question any marketer or chief executive officer (CEO) will ask. "How many do we have and how many can I get?" is a basic question in Business 101.

Table 3.1

Sample Product-Usage Table with Demographics

	Budweiser heavy user	
	Male base users (%)	Index
Age 21–34	35.6	139
Household income $50K<	57.9	115
Single	34.3	142
Education—No college	56.8	116

Source: Mediamark Research, Inc. 2004. Reprinted with permission.

Depending on the product or service with which you are involved, there is typically information available giving you a quantitative view of your customers. The information could be Nielsen (Nielsen Media Research) or IRI (Information Resources, Inc.) data in the packaged-goods world; or sales lists from a B2B (business-to-business) product; or checks, credit cards, warranty cards, or any other item that comes from a bill of sale.

Now that you know how many consumers you have, you will want to determine who they are demographically or what job title or function they might have if you are marketing a B2B good or service. In the consumer arena, there are a number of sources that can aid you in determining your target market. The standard tools available in the United States include MRI (Mediamark Research, Inc.), SMRB (Simmons Market Research Bureau), and Scarborough Research. All these sources offer robust databases that provide a complete demographic description about customers of thousands of products and services. Factors such as gender, age, income, education, geographic location, and number of children in the household are among the many factors you have at your fingertips. If you are working with a consumer packaged-goods manufacturer, there are more databases such as IRI or Nielsen that can aid in understanding who is buying your product. For many services and retailers, credit card companies can offer a wealth of data on who buys your product. Table 3.1 offers an example of a brand's demographic profile using MRI.

What Are Your Customers Like?

Determining who your customers are gives essentially basic but crucial information. As an account planner, you want to be able to dimensionalize the consumers who buy your brand. Once you have a handle on who they

Table 3.2

Typical Day-in-the-Life Tracking Chart

Time of day	Activity	Media contact opportunities
5 A.M.–7 A.M.	Wake up Get kids to school	Watch/listen morning news
7 A.M.–8 A.M.	Off to work	Listen to news/talk radio, exposed to out-of-home
8 A.M.–12 noon	At work	Check e-mail, research online, skim newspaper
12 noon–1 P.M.	A quick bite	Listen to news radio, check PDA for market updates
1 P.M.–5 P.M.	Back at work	Check online for stock updates, check mail, check magazines
5 P.M.–6 P.M.	Back at home	Listen to radio, exposed to out-of-home
6 P.M.–10 P.M.	Family time	Watch favorite TV shows to unwind with kids, surf Internet
10 P.M.–11 P.M.	Down time	Read magazine/newspaper articles
11 P.M.	Sleep	

are, the next step is to find out what they are like. Do they drive a Lexus or a Volkswagen Beetle? Do they vacation in Spain or in Branson, Missouri?

With all the secondary data that you have available telling you about your customer, you should use it to help create a timeline of a typical day in the life of your consumer. This will help media planners better understand how to develop a contact strategy and it will help copywriters get a better feel for their audience.

This type of exercise is also important for the client in a number of ways. By understanding what other items might appeal to this consumer, you may spark new thinking on a line extension to an existing product or for a new product to be developed. This information can also help marketers with more tactical decisions, such as timing of promotions or cross-promotional partners. Most "day-in-the-life" exercises use MRI and/or SMRB as the basis for much of this information. Using those databases, you can cross-tabulate your consumers with thousands of others' products, media usage, and various attitudinal statements that can be used to craft a typical "day-in-the-life" exercise (see Table 3.2).

From this exercise for an affluent banking customer, you quickly can see that the audience members have fragmented media habits and that every minute of their day is crammed full of activities. The implication of this information is that you will need to "cut to the chase" in terms of advertising in order to talk to this particular customer.

Why Do They Buy Your Product?

Okay, now you know who is buying your product and some of the things going on in their lives, but the issue separating insight from information is knowing the motivation of your customer. What need are you satisfying?

On the surface, understanding why someone buys your product may seem like a real "no brainer." If you are marketing toothpaste, you know people need to brush their teeth to keep them clean so they won't rot in their mouths. This is a pretty basic need, but they may also brush their teeth so they feel clean, which makes them feel healthy. Or they may brush their teeth so they will look good, so they will feel more confident when they go out. The "why" is sometimes an illusory question and sometimes raises more questions than it answers.

Physical and Psychological Needs

Human needs fall into two basic categories: physical and psychological (social). The basic physical needs are things like food, water, shelter, or heat. As long as a person's physical needs go unmet, there is really no reason to talk to a consumer about psychological buying motives. Even in today's modern society, many consumers don't have the basics. Unless you are marketing a luxury good, don't assume that the entire consumer market is not still interested in satisfying some of the basics.

A good example of this situation is in the auto industry. Talking about the roomy interior of the car will likely fall on deaf ears to someone who has to take the bus to work every day. For this transportation-challenged consumer, a low-cost payment plan is likely to be the most compelling reason to buy your car.

Physical needs tend to be the strongest needs a person has and they take precedence over psychological needs. As the physical needs are met, then a consumer will look to fulfill more complex needs.

The fundamental structure for looking at need assessment is Abraham Maslow's Hierarchy of Human Needs. Figure 3.1 illustrates Maslow's pyramid of needs. The bottom rung on the ladder is physical or physiological

Figure 3.1   **Maslow's Hierarchy of Human Needs**

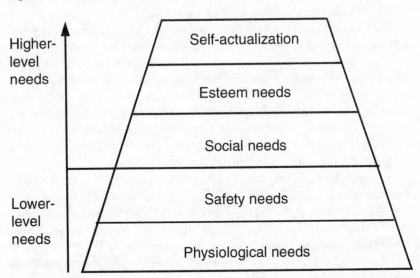

needs, which we have talked about. The next rung is safety and security; for example, this step may be the level that provides the motivation to buy insurance. The next rung up is social needs, reflecting the desire for affection and approval from others; this can include buying the right style of clothes or drinking the popular brand of beer. The next rung up the ladder is self-esteem: This is the feeling of accomplishment or self-respect or prestige: it might be buying a certain car to say you have arrived, or breaking ninety on the golf course. The final stage of the pyramid is self-actualization; it is at this stage where you seek self-improvement and balance in your life.

Maslow's Hierarchy of Human Needs is a foundation for need assessment and benefit segmentation in today's marketplace. While there are many need-based schemes, most are derived from Maslow's initial work.

Researching for Motivations

Delving into a consumer's psyche is not an easy thing to do. No one wants to admit there is some deep psychological reason why they buy a certain brand or product. Most of us want to give some rational explanation for why we buy what we buy. For example, a middle-age man who buys a Jaguar sure isn't doing it because it is a high-performance car, but it is the reason that he would tell you if you asked. How can we figure out what is the real motivation behind the purchase? There are a couple of key ways for an account planner to ferret out this information.

The first way is simply to observe the customer in his natural setting. Observational research has grown considerably in the past few years. This popular technique is called ethnographic research when a trained researcher, typically an anthropology-trained professional, spends time with a small group of customers in their homes or wherever they might be using the product. From an intimate setting, the researcher observes and asks questions of the consumers and their families about a range of topics, including why they buy a specific brand. This type of research can be very insightful because it gets at the heart of issues where most quantitative research cannot.

For example, observing how a mom and her family ate Manwich Sloppy Joes led to an insight about the brand that was manifested in the advertising. When looking at the nightly menus on the refrigerators of the homes they visited, researchers found that the nights they served Manwich were "fun nights." Probing this idea further, the researcher found Manwich night was the one "fun break" in an otherwise traditional meal-planning week. It was the time when the family could "kick back" and have fun together. This insight led to the creative strategy of executing "fun on a bun." While most food advertising focuses, and rightly so, on the food, Manwich was focused on the fun times that the food brought to the table.

Another popular qualitative research technique used to get after motivations is a projection technique where a researcher asks a respondent to bring in pictures or words describing a brand. By skillfully asking questions in a one-on-one setting, a researcher can uncover the deeper reasons into why someone might be buying the product. This research also sometimes uses a technique called "laddering," where the researcher leads the consumer from the more rational benefit to the more emotional benefit. Figure 3.2 demonstrates a "picture sort" using cars and trucks as the metaphor. If the brand is rugged, then the consumers might choose the pickup truck; if the brand is stylish, they might choose the sports car. The whole idea of these techniques is to get after deeper issues of the brand's link to the consumer.

The same is true of using word associations. The researcher is asking a consumer to match the brand's personality to a variety of words that might describe it. This technique offers the researcher a chance to engage the consumer in a deeper dialogue than just how much the consumer likes the brand. Figure 3.3 is an example of a word-association exercise.

There are even companies such as Sensory Logic that combine a one-on-one interview with a quantitative measure of facial expressions and galvanic skin response to give a numerical dimension to the emotional response.

Figure 3.2   **Picture Sort**

The power behind Sensory Logic's technique is that facial expressions are universal. There have been many studies confirming that people's facial reactions are the same from culture to culture. For example, people in China smile if something makes them happy just like people do in the United States. This universal truth goes for all of the basic emotions. Reading these facial expressions, then, can be a strong tool in unlocking a person's true reactions to a concept, an advertisement, or a person.

The latter are all great methods to garner some consumer insights. Because most business people want to make quantitative-based decisions, it is standard practice to use a combination of qualitative and quantitative methods when analyzing consumer motivations. Quantitative studies, also called need-based segmentation studies, are used to classify consumers based on how they use a particular brand. For example, a fast-food restaurant chain might have Convenience Cathy as one segment. She may be a single, working mom who is so busy that she is totally convenience-driven in her decision choices. Conversely, there may be Craving Carl who simply craves hamburgers and must have a "burger fix" at least once a week. From this type of segmentation work, you can begin to develop marketing targets for your brand; see Figure 3.4 for an example.

It should be noted that quantitative studies of needs are only going to get deeper into more rational motivations like the ones we discussed above. Things

Figure 3.3 **Word Association**

Family-oriented	Cool	Glamorous
Small-town	Young	Good-looking
Conventional	Lively	Pretentious
Blue-collar	Outgoing	Sophisticated
All-American	Adventurous	
Sincere	Unique	Feminine
Real	Humorous	Smooth
Ethical	Surprising	Sexy
Thoughtful	Artistic	Gentle
Caring	Fun	
Original	Independent	Masculine
Genuine	Contemporary	Western
Ageless	Innovative	Active
Classic	Aggressive	Athletic
Old-fashioned		
Sentimental	Hardworking	Rugged
Friendly	Secure	Strong
Warm	Efficient	No-nonsense
Happy	Trustworthy	
	Careful	
Trendy	Technical	Leader
Exciting	Corporate	Confident
Off-beat	Serious	Influential
Flashy		
Provocative		

like convenience, or even basic urges such a taste or flavor, are still more in the realm of rational motivations rather than more emotional motivations such as "feeling good about oneself" or " being one of the guys to fit in." This is why you should mix qualitative and quantitative measures together when you are trying to understand what makes a customer tick.

Product Involvement

As you shape your strategies for understanding what makes your customer think and act, you should determine early on what level of involvement the consumer has with your category or product.

This thinking applies a level of intensity to the feelings someone might have about your brand. For example, Harley Davidson riders might tattoo the brand on their arms. Now that is high involvement! On the other hand, how emotionally involved will you get with a can of green beans? You've

Figure 3.4   **Need-based Segmentation: Cooking Spray Category**

never seen the Jolly Green Giant tattooed on some housewife's arm. Actually, the thought of that is rather frightening.

So the more strongly consumers are driven to satisfy their needs, the more likely they are to become emotionally involved with the brand. Consumers who are motivated to project a certain social image may be more involved with one brand than with other brands.

The interesting thing about involvement is that it does not follow Maslow's Hierarchy of Needs. The basic need for heat in your home is a core physical need but it is doubtful that most consumers are emotionally attached to their electric or gas utility. On the other hand, self-esteem needs have very high emotional attachments. Consumers may feel passionately about a brand of make-up, a brand of clothes, or a certain car, but not care one iota about who provides them with electrical power.

One exercise you should try with your brand is to gauge its involvement or intensity. In 1985, Judith Zaichkowsky designed a useful Involvement Tool. She developed a twenty-question survey assessing the interest level in a specific category using a seven-point scale, from 1 being low interest to 7 being high interest. A score of 140 (20 × 7) would be a maximum score and would be "off the charts" in terms of involvement. Her study of fifteen categories revealed a mean score of 89.55. Automobiles were the most involving of the categories she studied, while instant coffee and breakfast cereal were the least involving. By combining intensity with the level of need, you can begin to add some dimension to the category you are studying (see Figure 3.5).

Figure 3.5   **Motivation and Intensity Grid**

important	1	2	3	4	5	6	7	unimportant
of no concern	1	2	3	4	5	6	7	of concern to me
irrelevant	1	2	3	4	5	6	7	relevant
means a lot to me	1	2	3	4	5	6	7	means nothing to me
useless	1	2	3	4	5	6	7	useful
valuable	1	2	3	4	5	6	7	worthless
trivial	1	2	3	4	5	6	7	fundamental
beneficial	1	2	3	4	5	6	7	not beneficial
matters to me	1	2	3	4	5	6	7	doesn't matter
uninterested	1	2	3	4	5	6	7	interested
significant	1	2	3	4	5	6	7	insignificant
vital	1	2	3	4	5	6	7	superfluous
boring	1	2	3	4	5	6	7	interesting
unexciting	1	2	3	4	5	6	7	exciting
appealing	1	2	3	4	5	6	7	unappealing
mundane	1	2	3	4	5	6	7	fascinating
essential	1	2	3	4	5	6	7	nonessential
undesirable	1	2	3	4	5	6	7	desirable
wanted	1	2	3	4	5	6	7	unwanted
not needed	1	2	3	4	5	6	7	needed

Source: J.L. Zaichkowsky, "Measuring the Involvement Construct," *Journal of Consumer Research* 12, no. 3 (1985): pp. 341–352. Used with permission of the University of Chicago Press.

The Consumer's Story

Every consumer has a story, just as every brand has a story. One way to look at consumers is through the stories they tell. We all construct the stories of our lives. We use these stories to build our identities. The story of our identity answers such questions as: Who am I? What do I want? Where am I? Where am I going? By listening to consumer stories we can explore the ways in which brands enter consumer lives.

As we have mentioned previously in this chapter, research and planning have embraced ethnography, which is the close observation of consumers' lives. One aspect of ethnographic research is not only to observe consumers but also to listen to their stories. Allowing consumers to tell their stories is a way to get after the truth about consumer behavior and attitudes, which traditional research cannot accomplish.

For example, the majority of brand research asks relatively abstract questions such as:

- How favorable is your attitude to Coca-Cola?
- How much do you like to drink Coke?
- How well does Coke satisfy your thirst?

While consumers will answer these questions, the resulting answers can be largely meaningless. Most managers struggle to find meaning behind a 6.5 versus 7.2 on a scale of 1 to 10 regarding how well Coke (in this hypothetical example) quenches one's thirst; that would be a range of only seven units out of a total possible 100 ($7.2 - 6.5 = 0.7/10.0$). Quantitative research can be very effective at benchmarking attitudes but leaves a lot to be desired in terms of getting at the motivations and strengths of a brand relationship with a consumer. Our previous example of Coca-Cola illustrates this point very well. Coke had conducted mountains of research with thousands of consumers to support its change from old Coke to new Coke. While the data supported consumers liking the new taste, it did not delve into deeper bonds consumers had with the brand. As a result, new Coke failed and the company quickly brought back old Coke as Coca-Cola Classic.

To get into the consumers' minds, you need to get at the underlying story on which their values are based. This can be accomplished through the use of a well-prepared ethnographic researcher, establishing an atmosphere of trust and then exploring the topic with much more open-ended questions inviting the consumer to tell stories. The following is such an example, again, using Coke as the hypothetical case.

- "After I tell you about the last time I drank a soft drink, would you like to tell me about your experience drinking a Coke?"
- "Have you had any experiences while drinking a Coke? Can you tell us about those experiences? Do you recall how you felt about drinking Coke? Can you tell me the reactions of your friends?"
- "What have you heard of experiences other people were having while drinking Coca-Cola?"

This type of interviewing process may last for a half an hour or more. As it continues, the interviewer will get deeper and deeper into the psyche of the consumers' stories and how the brand in question fits into their lives. The richness of this exercise can help management better understand the emotional underpinnings of the brand. It can give the advertising agency's creative group a much deeper sense of what nerve endings can be exposed throughout the advertising creative process. It gives both the businessperson and the communicator a richer sense of not only who the consumers are, but how the particular product or service fits within the context of their lives.

To summarize, understanding the consumer is the most important item for an account planner. It is your reason to exist. In understanding the consumer, you need to tackle this task from both a quantitative and a qualitative perspective. From this analysis will come both the business strategy and the communications strategy. Along the way, there will come consumer insight aiding in the growth of the brand.

Review Questions

1. What kinds of useful information can a market researcher learn from association techniques? From interviews? From logic? From focus groups?
2. What are the advantages of telephone research? Of personal interviews? Of mail questionnaires? What are the disadvantages of each?
3. What is the difference between quantitative research and qualitative research?
4. How is research used by advertising account planners?

Discussion Questions

1. What are the problems of understanding the consumers of a product or service? How can these obstacles be overcome?
2. Compare the usefulness of statistical reliability against sensory logic and personal insights.
3. On what basis can a marketer segment an audience?
4. What are the problems with quantifying consumer research? Which consumer attributes are most easily quantified? Which are most difficult to quantify?

Exercises

1. Select a certain product or service brand. Then develop the questions to be used in a research questionnaire to gain insights and information about the consumers of that brand. Test your questionnaire on another person to help determine how questions are answered and how they may be misunderstood or misinterpreted.
2. Form a small focus group and conduct research on the same product or service brand. What information can be learned from a focus group that cannot be obtained through the use of a questionnaire? What can be learned through a questionnaire that cannot be gained from a focus group?

CBC Case Study

Review the CBC case from Chapter 1.

1. If you have access to data from syndicated market research firms such as SMRB or MRI, look up the soft drink category. What can you say for certain about the consumers of soft drinks, their demographic characteristics and their media habits? How are heavy users defined? How are the characteristics of heavy users different from those of light users?
2. Develop and test a questionnaire for learning more about the consumers of soft drinks.
3. Develop and test focus group research to find out what are the key reasons and benefits for consuming soft drinks.

Additional Sources

Foxall, Gordon. *Understanding Consumer Choice*. New York: Palgrave Macmillan, 2005.

Juster, Thomas F. *Consumer Buying Intentions and Purchase Probability: An Experiment in Survey Design*. New York: Columbia University Press, 1966.

Mancini, Marc. *Connecting with Customers: How to Sell, Service, and Market the Travel Product*. Upper Saddle River, NJ: Prentice Hall, 2003.

Marder, Eric. *Laws of Choice: Predicting Customer Behavior*. New York: Free Press, 1997.

Stinnett, Bill. *Think Like Your Customer: A Winning Strategy to Maximize Sales by Understanding and Influencing How and Why Your Customers Buy*. New York: McGraw-Hill, 2004.

Chapter 4

Defining the Target Market

The most important aspect of your role as account planner is to determine to whom you should direct your marketing efforts. Understanding who the consumers are, what they do, and why they buy your product gives you the foundation to define your target markets and groups.

Start with Marketing Objectives

Identifying to whom you should market seems like common sense. But isn't just identifying who buys the product enough? Perhaps. If your strategy is to get the current customer to purchase your product more often, then, by all means, you should focus your attention on the existing customer base.

But sometimes the existing user isn't the purchaser of the brand. For example, while tweens and teens are the largest consumers of Chef Boyardee, they are nowhere near the grocery store and unable to buy the brand. Mom is the purchaser of the product and as this brand found out in the 1990s, if you don't talk to Mom, sales go south rather fast.

It is important to start with the behavior that you feel you can affect. There are only a limited number of ways to grow a brand. We have discussed one method, that is, to get those consumers to use the brand more often. This is called increasing the buy rate and it is very useful if you are dealing with a packaged-goods brand.

If you are marketing a B2B service, the way to grow sales might be to sell additional services to the same client. For example, if you are the brand manager for Dell Computers, you may use your relationship with the IT (information technology) group at a client's firm to sell them servers, laptops, and a service agreement.

The other common approach to growth is to attract new users to the brand. This is often called a penetration strategy. One way to accomplish this aim is to get competitive users to switch to your brand. This situation is certainly the case in mature categories like laundry detergent, where Tide fights it out with Cheer for control of the aisle. The irony in the laundry detergent category is that both Tide and Cheer are owned and marketed by

Procter & Gamble. Or you might try to increase the penetration level of a certain demographic group that is under-represented in your base. For example, Hispanics may be an emerging group on whom you may want to put more marketing pressure to stimulate increased sales.

Another method to increase penetration is to "increase the pie," or expand the category. One method within this framework is to reach out to traditional nonusers of a brand. For example, senior citizens may not be traditional purchasers of rap music, but you have an insight that they can feel closer to their grandchildren if they buy the latest rap CD for them. Another method to increase the category is to actually change the category in which you compete. For example, Arm & Hammer baking soda changed its category from baking to odor removal to home remedies, all with the same box of baking soda.

Understanding how the brand can grow is the key to developing a marketing target. The first step to helping define the growth target is to define the target in behavioral terms.

Target Triangle

There are three angles to understanding the interplay of a target market. The first and most obvious target is someone who buys the product; this person is called the brand purchaser. The brand purchaser, as we have discussed, may or may not be the person who is actually consuming or using the product. There are numerous packaged-goods examples of this where a mom is buying cereal, canned pasta, cookies, or chips for her children. In the B2B arena, there are also many cases where the purchaser of a good or service may not be the person who is actually using it. The chief financial officer (CFO) may arrange for a deal with FedEx to ship all the company's packages, but the administrative assistant may be the one actually using the service.

The second target is a person who is using the good or service—the brand user. While the brand user may or may not be the actual purchaser of the product, more often than not, they are typically one and the same.

The third element of the target triangle is the purchase influencer. A purchase influencer is someone who neither buys the brand nor uses it, but influences the person who is the brand purchaser. For example, a father may influence the purchase of an automobile by his grown daughter. She may consult him as to the most reliable car or dealership, but she will be the one actually making the purchase. We often see purchase influencers in the consumer arena with larger-ticket items such as cars or items where expertise is required, as in buying a surround-sound stereo system. The

Figure 4.1   **Target Triangle**

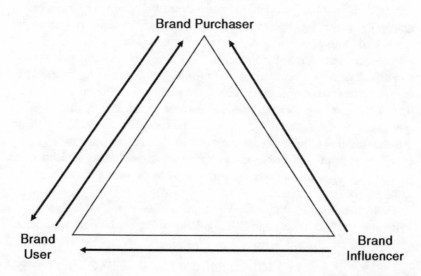

role of the purchase influencer is particularly strong in B2B purchases. For example, the old phrase "Nobody ever got fired for buying IBM" was born out of the purchase influencer's role of CEOs who were not technology savvy. While they may not understand technology, they felt comfortable with a venerable brand name like IBM so they would influence their CIOs to purchase this brand of computer hardware.

As an account planner, you must understand the interplay of the target triangle (see Figure 4.1). Each brand or company will have a unique set of purchasers, users, and/or influencers. Some purchases are very straightforward; others are more complex and involve all three parts of the target triangle. In these cases, it is up to the account planner to help sort out the appropriate weights given to assign to each of these groups. In your account planner role, as you understand the dynamics of the purchase behavior, you will add more layers of understanding to develop a marketing target.

Defining the Target by Usage

We have discussed the three types of people who may impact the purchase of a product or service. While weighing the importance of these three types of people is important, it pales in comparison to understanding those customers who make up a disproportionate amount of usage.

One classic way in which many marketers define their target market is based on usage. There are secondary research sources as well as point-of-sale information services that help identify heavy, medium, or light users. These monikers correspond to the frequency of usage, with heavy being the most frequent and light being the least frequent.

The "Pareto principle" states that 20 percent of consumers represent 80 percent of the purchases of a brand. While this 80 : 20 rule may or may not apply to the brand or category you are studying, there is typically some sort of heavy-user segment or purchase-dynamic activity with any brand.

Obviously, retaining heavy users is crucial to a brand's survival. For every one heavy user you lose, you would need to add four other users to make up the lost volume based on the "Pareto principle." That is one tough assignment. This type of analysis is also telling in terms of comparing your heavy users to the product category. If teens are heavy users of cereal yet your cereal brand doesn't attract teens, this could signal an opportunity for you to increase sales to this segment.

Going back to the ways of growing your business, moving a light user up to a heavy user is a common strategy marketers use to grow their sales. So, defining your target market by usage has a lot of business implications. It can also have media strategy implications as well; if the brand strategy is to increase usage among heavy/medium users, then media plans should be developed to reflect that target market.

As an account planner, you can use the target triangle and the usage definitions of targeting as important aids relating to the business side of the brand equation. The brand's management and marketing teams will be focused on these numerical ways of defining the target market. This approach spills over into the advertising arena with media strategy that is highly quantitative in nature. Now the challenge becomes how to reconcile the business data with consumer needs and motivations.

Defining the Brand's Need State

The essence of any brand and consumer bond is how that brand satisfies a consumer need. Thus, as an account planner, you have a major role to help brand management identify consumer-need states now and trends that might affect those need states in the future.

The best way to understand a need state is within the context of the brand and the demographic or usage based target. Here are a few examples to think about:

Michelin Tires: For safety-conscious parents with young children.

American Express: For prestige-conscious frequent travelers who seek special recognition.

Chef Boyardee: For busy working moms who want to feed their children real food, real fast.

IBM: For risk-averse executives who have IT responsibility.

If you pay attention to advertising in any medium, you can begin to spot the needs the brand is trying to address. Tapping into an emotional need is the cornerstone to linking the brand to the consumer. The brands named above have captured that emotional high ground. Many other brands have not. Identifying the consumer need state is paramount to developing a marketing target. It is also the key that aids the advertising copywriter and art director in crafting a compelling message that hits your target bull's-eye.

In your analysis of the consumer, you should ask yourself, "What does the customer really need?" In the case of a business manager who is buying a number of computer servers, his overwhelming personal need is not to make a mistake. He is responsible for investing a lot of time and money. His reputation is on the line and he may have a family to feed. IBM fills that personal need by being a safe choice. However, this is not the only reason a manager may buy technology. There are other managers who are willing to take a risk if it means they will gain an advantage or be perceived as innovative. For this group of strivers, IBM may not be the answer. If this group becomes larger than the risk-averse group, then IBM would need to ensure it has the perceived superior technology so it could capture the purchases from the innovators.

The same is true of consumer products. The difference between Visa and American Express is ubiquity versus exclusivity. Visa is "Everywhere you want to be." It is everything to everyone. American Express, on the other hand, is all about exclusivity. "Membership has its rewards" is the perfect mantra for the exclusive claim of American Express. They are two basically similar products that are positioned and that appeal to very different consumer need states. As you work with a client, it is important to note there will be different need states available into which you can tap. The trick is to pick the one that fits your brand.

The Marketing Target

Now it is time to pull it all together. The elements of a marketing target are an understanding of whom you want to influence: the brand purchaser, the

Table 4.1

Marketing Target

Demographics	Male, 21 to 34[a]
Current Usage Habits	Drinks 3+ beers per week[a]
Need State	Be one of the guys[b]
Target Market	Young, male, frequent beer drinker who wants to be one of the guys

[a]*Source:* Mediamark Research, Inc.; Simmons Market Research Bureau; Nielsen Media Research; Scarborough Research; Information Resources, Inc.
[b]*Source:* Qualitative research.

brand user, or the brand influencer, along with their demographics, usage, and mindset.

Table 4.1 is an example of a marketing target that pulls these components together. Of the marketing target components that we have discussed, the need state is by far the most important. The demographics and usage habits of the target are merely background contexts for the need state. The need state is really the bait to attract the target to your product.

The question you should ask yourself after developing a marketing target is, "To whom am I marketing?" Once that is agreed upon, you can then begin to direct creative groups and media groups to tackle the question of "How can I reach them?" and "What do I say to them to make them behave the way I would like them to?"

In crafting a marketing target, it is important to be precise. This selectivity may go against the grain of the company or even brand management who may want any mom to buy their cereal. They may ask, "Why should I limit myself to this tight definition?" The answer is that in today's overcommunicated society, you must be precise in your targeting or no one will pay attention to you.

It is up to you, as the account planner, to pull the marketing target together. The marketing target is the most crucial aspect to brand positioning, advertising creative development, and media planning. So take your time in developing the marketing target that will yield the best business results by being the one that taps into a core consumer value that represents a need state.

Personalize the Target

You now have your marketing target and you may be feeling pretty smug. You know the target group's demographics and its usage behavior and you have done your homework about the target's needs and motivations. You may well ask, "What more can I do?" The answer is, plenty!

You should constantly work to help humanize or personalize the target market. You should try to get the target market defined in a phrase or a name. This process helps give the information some context and is an easy "handle" for anyone on the marketing or creative teams to grasp quickly. Whether you get to invent a fun name like "Pressure Cooker Mom" or "Beer-Drinking Bubba," it is important for the brand group and the creative group to have a single person with whom to identify when you are developing your marketing communications. Any effective piece of communication should be written on a personal level. So, the more you personalize the target market, the more apt you are to get communications that connect with the consumer at an emotional level.

In their book *Creating Brand Loyalty,* Richard Czerniawski and Michael Maloney do an excellent job of discussing how to define a target market and how to bring it to a personal level. Table 4.2 is an example of the Tide target market from their book. This approach adds a number of personal dimensions to the target market.

Consumer Narrative

Another way to personalize the target market is to draw upon our storytelling methods to develop a consumer narrative. The consumer narrative takes all the information that you have gleaned about the target market and puts it into a story format. From the Tide example in Table 4.2, you can see that Mary Beth Williams is a very busy mother. She is taking care of kids while keeping her husband's books. This gal is working herself to the bone. So, we might call her "Multitask Mary." She is looking for something to help her with the myriad of chores and decisions that she makes daily in her whirlwind life. This is where Tide comes in. No matter what gets on the clothes, Tide gets it out, first time, every time. In Multitask Mary's world, there just isn't time for second chances. So, Tide becomes one of those small heroes to Mary for making her hectic life just a little bit easier.

Now, wouldn't you feel great reading this story about Multitask Mary if you were the Tide brand manager? You're darned right you would. You would feel the empathy for her and her plight. If you were the copywriter assigned to this brand, it would stimulate you to write copy that motivates her. Creating a story about the consumer of the brand is one way of connecting the customer to the creative and the brand groups.

In the consumer narrative, we all create stories about how we are sup-

Table 4.2

Target Customer Profile, Tide Retail Consumer Example

Name: Mary Beth Williams	
Gender: Female	Age: 38
Marital status (married to/number of years): John (8)–2nd marriage	
Children (ages): Tricia (17), Billy (15), John Jr. (18), James (15), Melissa (6), Rob and Ed (4)	

Occupation	Full-time caretaker, part-time bookkeeper for husband John's roofing business
Education	Regina High School
Personal auto	Ford Bronco
Currently working on	Picking up after children!
My favorite leisure activity is	I don't have time for leisure
I stay home to watch (on TV)	"Rosanne," "Home Improvement," "As the World Turns"
Last good book I read	I don't have time to read books!
The newspaper/magazines I usually read include	*People, Readers Digest, Good Housekeeping, Enquirer*
My favorite music/performer is	Classic Rock (The Eagles)
The last vacation I took was	Last summer we drove to and camped in Yosemite
I love to shop for	Earrings
My favorite shopping place is	Flea markets and garage sales
What my friends say about me (when I'm not in their presence) is	If she doesn't slow down she is going to drive herself into the ground
If I could change one thing about myself it would be	I would have gone to college
A really good evening to me is	Go out alone with John to either a movie or dinner (just get away from the house and kids)
My dream life is	To win the lottery and not have to do a damn thing
The reason(s) I choose Tide (vs. competitive brands) is	Tide gets even the dirtiest clothes clean (and I can tell you my husband and the twins really get their clothes dirty) without damaging the fabric so we can all look our best. Also, I can usually buy it on special.

posed to act. Moms are supposed to be supportive and selfless. A teenager's coming of age is like an endless series of adventures. And people's stories are also colored by how and when they grew up. Different generations look at the world through different eyes and experiences. For example, "baby boomers" have always had a spiritual quest for the meaning in their lives while members of "Generation X" have been more interested in the pursuit of balance in their lives. As you paint a picture of the target market, you must realize that it is important to understand not only who the targets are and why they are buying your brand, but also where they are in their personal journeys in life.

Summary

In this chapter and in the preceding one, you saw that in defining the target market, you first need to understand the target's demographics and usage. To determine these facts, there are many sources the brand group or media planning group can use to define these characteristics. From there, you must do the hard work to uncover the consumers' need states or motivations on why they buy the brand. You might need to field primary research to understand these underlying issues.

Finally, when you have the information all together, you should make sure that the marketing target means more business for the brand. Then you should personalize the target market so you can create the most focused communications possible.

Review Questions

1. From a marketing perspective, what are the limits of demographic segmentation?
2. What other kinds of segmentation are available to marketers? In what situations might they be more valuable than demographics?
3. What kinds of problems might be incurred in trying to collect demographic information from consumers? What kinds of problems might be incurred in trying to collect other (nondemographic) information from consumers?
4. How is selling to an individual different from selling to a group?

Discussion Questions

1. What are the different roles in the purchase process of the influencer, the purchaser, and the user of a product or service?

2. Make a list of as many types of demographic characteristics as possible. How is each useful and how is each limited in its application to marketing?
3. What are the problems in gathering accurate information from consumers?
4. What are the advantages and disadvantages of each of three ways for a company to increase its sales: increase usage; add more users; add more items to buy.

Exercises

What are the characteristics of heavy, medium, and light viewers of broadcast television? Try to gather this information from standard syndicated research sources (such as Simmons of MRI) or from searching for marketing literature. Then conduct your own original research to gather the same kinds of information. How do your findings compare with the standardized findings?

CBC Case Study

Go back to Chapter 1 and review the CBC case. Then, define the most logical targets for the major competitors of CBC.
Now do the same for CBC.

1. What differences, if any, did you discover?
2. How could CBC use this information in its marketing programs?
3. Define the usage habits of CBC's target group.
4. Compile a target customer profile for CBC.
5. Now develop a statement that defines the need state for customers of CBC.

Additional Sources

Clifton, Rita, and John Simmons. *Brands and Branding*. Princeton, NJ: Bloomberg Press, 2004.
Czerniawski, Richard D., and Michael W. Maloney. *Creating Brand Loyalty: The Management of Power Positioning and Really Great Advertising*. New York: AMACOM, 1999.
Dowling, Grahame. *The Art & Science of Marketing*. London: Oxford University Press, 2004.
Ragas, Matthew W., and Bolivar J. Bueno. *The Power of Cult Branding: How 9 Magnetic Brands Turned Customers into Loyal Followers (and Yours Can, Too!)*. Roseville, CA: Prima Venture, 2000.

Chapter 5
Defining the Benefit

There is a saying, "Nobody wants to buy a drill. What they really want is a hole." Consumers want to know what is in it for them. Frankly, they couldn't care less about what you do unless it means something good for them. Consumers are sure a selfish lot. This is true regardless of the buying situation. Whether it is buying a product or a service, or deciding on a retailer or a business good or service, customers want to know the benefit and not just the attribute.

Getting to the benefit seems like a fairly easy exercise, but for many companies, demonstrating a true customer benefit can be very difficult. This problem is particularly true for companies such as retailers, business-to-business marketers, and service providers. Amassing attributes is what they do. Their goal in building a company is all tied up in adding services or products, systems, and channels of distribution. While CEOs of these companies understand the distinction between an attribute and a benefit, they are very focused on the attribute side of the equation.

On the other hand, for consumer packaged-goods companies, getting to the product's benefit is the lifeblood of their existence. They are very consumer-focused and brand-centric. If there weren't any special benefit of one toothpaste versus another, you would just buy the one that might be the least expensive. But, there are tons of toothpastes on the market. Some make your teeth cleaner. Some whiten your teeth. Some make your breath feel fresher. Some taste like cherries. There are benefits galore. The majority of packaged-goods marketers are constantly looking to create a new product feature that can be turned into a consumer benefit.

Suppose you are the CEO of a *Fortune* 500 company; what accounting firm do you pick? With all the accounting scandals of recent times, selecting an accounting firm is a high-stakes decision. It is also much more difficult to discern the difference between companies than it is to discern the difference between products or individuals. The same is true for many service businesses. Try discerning the difference between one hospital system and another. What is the difference between one law firm or one advertising agency and another? Retailing is another area where it is truly difficult to find clear consumer benefits. What is the difference between one gas station and another? Or what is the difference between one furniture store and another?

It seems that the higher the stakes in terms of costs and potential for a large amount of personal disappointment, the less likely it is that a clear consumer benefit will be evident. As an account planner, it is your job to help companies understand the customer's point of view regarding their brands, services, or companies and to help hone their attributes into meaningful benefits.

What Is an Attribute?

All products, services, retailers, and companies have unique attributes that make up their businesses. If they did not have something of substance, they would have no reason to exist. Attributes are how we compare brands or businesses. This is why businesses are driven to produce unique attributes. They are constantly trying to differentiate themselves from their competitors. Product attributes for packaged-goods products are typically called features. Other businesses, such as retailers, service businesses, and business-to-business marketers, typically have attributes that are born out of unique business practices. While a packaged-good product might have a unique selling proposition (USP), a retailer, service, or business-to-business marketer may have a unique business proposition.

In Table 5.1, there is a list of common attributes for different categories of business. Let's take a look at the products. Product attributes are easiest for us to discern and are most common in our lives as consumers. For example, a floor cleaner may add lemon to mask the ammonia smell of the cleaning liquid; the lemony smell is a product feature. Most mustard brands have gone to a squeeze bottle that has a true squirt nozzle; this is a packaging feature. M&M's candies come in various sizes, shapes, and colors; again, these are all product features. We can go down the list of common product attributes and think of everyday products that have unique tastes, sounds, shapes, and smells.

Now let's take a look at retailing. Most retailers define themselves by the merchandise they carry and sell. Some are in business based on delivering just merchandise, such as Gap, the clothing store. The Gap is all about delivering the basic look. The company's stores reflect the simplicity of the merchandise. Look at these standard retail attributes; you have surely seen them in action. Do you remember the first twenty-four-hour grocery store? The 7-Eleven convenience store brand was first named after the long hours

Table 5.1

Common Attributes

Products	Retail
Substance	Store design
Structure	Hours open
Color	Merchandise
Shape	Delivery
Texture	Sales personnel
Sound	Pricing (EDLP vs. sales)
Taste	Logistics
Odor	
Packaging	
Ingredients	
Patent	

B2B	Service
Patent	Customer service
Customer service	Geographic coverage
Distribution	Price
Unique process or method	Distribution/delivery
Price	Unique process/method
Area of expertise	
Geographic coverage	

it kept. Then other convenience stores had to stay open twenty-four hours to compete. Other concepts, such as the dollar stores (e.g., Dollar General and Dollar Store) have taken the price attribute as their claim to fame. The number one furniture retailer in the country built his business on same-day delivery. While other furniture stores made customers wait months for their orders, Gallery Furniture in Houston, Texas, developed a method for same-day delivery. This unique approach to business now helps the store generate more than $100 million in sales from a single location. Now that is one powerful attribute.

Many service-based companies began as a result of developing a unique attribute or business method. FedEx used a central-hub system to deliver packages overnight. Until FedEx launched its service, American Airlines and other carriers dominated this rapid package-delivery market; they never recovered from FedEx's business entry. Another service business, Motel 6, defined its business on a $6-a-night stay; the price has now crept up past $30 a night, but Motel 6 is still known as an inexpensive motel.

Northern Trust specializes in providing financial support to high-networth individuals; the firm has built a customer-service model that offers a suite of services that extremely wealthy individuals may need, ranging from traditional banking to more esoteric services such as philanthropy and complex trusts. Northern Trust is carving out a point of difference in the field of financial services. Those services having a unique business proposition or method are the ones that are most successful.

One area that doesn't get the publicity of these attribute categories is in the world of business-to-business marketing. Yet businesses are developed every day based on unique attributes or business propositions. One such business is Administaff. The company provides benefits to small businesses. The unique twist is that it offers firms to place their employees on Administaff's payroll. By consolidating numerous small businesses on one payroll, Administaff is able to gain a price advantage in dealing with health insurance and other employee benefits that have much greater costs than any small business could on its own.

Matlock Tools sells tools only to construction workers. To provide a special service, the staff drives tool vans to job sites and sells the tools right out of the van. Cisco Systems provides the routers that help move information from one computer or server to another; their special patents make them a leader in this rapidly changing technology field.

The point behind understanding attributes is this: It is what the business is focused on. As you have seen from the above examples, you can build a strong business on a unique attribute or business method. As an account planner, it is your job to help that business make the leap between offering a business attribute and offering a consumer benefit.

Attribute Versus Benefit

The customer benefit is what the attribute does for the customers. It is the consumer's reward. Again, from a consumer standpoint, the attributes don't do anything worthwhile unless there is a specific benefit attached to them. From a business-building standpoint, you can build a successful business based on a unique attribute or business model, but you can only build a strong brand or strong piece of communication based on a strong benefit.

To reiterate, what a product, service, or business does for the consumer is called a benefit. In many marketing textbooks, it is also called a functional benefit because it describes what the brand does or how it functions or performs in ways that benefit the customer. Most marketers just call it a benefit unless they are referencing an emotional benefit, which we will talk about a little later in this chapter.

For now, let's discuss the functional benefit. It is probably the most frequently used type of benefit in brand positioning and in advertising copy. If you have the first of a kind or new product "news," then the functional benefit may be the best thing to promote. For example, if you are the first hybrid car to run on gas and electricity, you may want to promote the functional benefit of getting seventy-five miles to a gallon of gas. In today's economic environment, where gasoline prices keep rising, this cost benefit is a pretty compelling message. If McDonald's introduces a nineteen-cent hamburger, it doesn't take a genius to figure out it's a good deal. The functional benefit of this offer is that you can eat a complete meal for under a buck. Now that sounds good when you are pinching pennies.

In Table 5.2, we have listed a series of products, goods, and services possessing unique attributes. We have listed the corresponding functional benefits. Let's walk through the examples to see how the categories differ in terms of turning a business attribute into a consumer benefit.

As we have mentioned previously, the package-goods arena is the easiest in which to discern benefits because a successful packaged-goods manufacturer is looking for consumer benefits. In the example, we have selected Hunt's tomato products. Hunt's is the leader in canned tomato products. As you can see, the firm's products have some solid attributes. They have 100 percent ACV (all-commodity volume), which is a packaged-good term for grocery distribution. In Hunt's case, all the grocery stores carry their products, so the benefit is that no matter where you shop, you will find their products. Hunt's also has a taste benefit; they select only vine-ripened tomatoes, which are the best-tasting. Hunt's has a health benefit as well; tomatoes contain Lycopene, which has been proven to be a natural source of antioxidants, helping prevent certain forms of cancer. One other benefit that Hunt's brings to consumers is that the brand has more than twenty varieties of products, so the benefit is that you can find just the right product that makes the meal you want delicious.

Just looking at this example, as an account planner, you could envision a number of ways to communicate the benefits of Hunt's. You could focus on taste, with the vine-ripened tomatoes telling the story that they are the best canned tomato on the market. Or you may direct your efforts to capitalize on the growing senior population with a health message. Perhaps you would be wise to communicate the variety of dishes that are easy to make with Hunt's products. Depending upon your objective, you might favor one approach over another.

Let's take a look at our retail example with a leading home-improvement retailer, Home Depot. The firm has a number of great business attributes that have made it very successful. It has put into place a low-price

Table 5.2

Attribute to Functional Benefit

Consumer Product: Hunt's Tomato	
Attributes	**Functional benefit**
100% ACV	Find it in any store
Made with vine-ripened tomatoes	Fresh-tasting tomatoes
Contains lycopene	Natural source of antioxidants
Over 20 varieties	Fits whatever you are cooking

Retailer: Home Depot	
Attributes	**Functional benefit**
Low-price guarantee	Always get best price
Hire former tradesmen as personnel	Expert advice
Carry name-brand merchandise	Find the brands I am familiar with
Deliver to job site	Convenient, saves time

Service: Southwest Airlines	
Attributes	**Functional benefit**
Fleet of planes all same model, which makes for easy service	Reliable service
Fly to close-in city airports	Convenient business travel
Low everyday fares	Inexpensive travel
Encourage flight attendants to have fun	Pleasant experience

Business-to-Business: Waste Management	
Attributes	**Functional benefit**
Only national company for hauling and landfills	Take care of my needs no matter how large my company becomes
All landfills are EPA certified	My waste will be in compliance with government regulations
Largest recycler in the United States	Establish and execute my recycling program
Use landfills to make methane gas to fuel their fleets	Environmentally conscious and innovative

guarantee, meaning it will match any price on the same item if a customer sees it advertised lower somewhere else. Wal-Mart has used the low-price attribute as its "killer attribute" for years. So now, most other "big-box" retailers use a low-price guarantee to combat Wal-Mart and other discount operations.

Home Depot has also distinguished itself from the competition by hiring former tradesmen as sales personnel. For average homeowners, finding someone who can give the proper advice and recommend all the right materials to get the job done is a strong consumer benefit. For the commercial trades, Home Depot has a separate checkout area and will deliver to the job site. Thus, the company is making it as convenient as possible for the contractors, saving them time and money.

It may come as no big surprise that Home Depot has run advertising for years showing their salespeople helping homeowners solve their problems. While Home Depot also advertises certain merchandise at selective price points, their umbrella advertising campaign of "You can do it. We can help" emphasizes the function benefit.

Service organizations such as Southwest Airlines have similar characteristics to retailers. Both kinds of firms require large investments in personnel, and people are the ones delivering the product or service. For Home Depot, the product may be showing a homeowner how to complete a project, and for Southwest Airlines the product is travel to a certain destination.

Southwest Airlines has revolutionized airline travel with some unusual business practices. Unlike other airlines, Southwest flies only one type of aircraft. This uniformity has become a huge competitive advantage for the airline. It makes the maintenance easier, holds down costs, and increases reliability. Southwest also holds down costs through short-haul trips, no food, and no first-class section, which spreads out the flight attendants throughout the airplane to take better care of passengers. All this allows Southwest to offer low fares. To balance its penchant for low costs, the airline encourages its flight attendants to be irreverent. So while not getting the extras could be a point of annoyance for business travelers, it is actually kind of fun to fly on Southwest Airlines. This is also what Southwest chooses to advertise to counterbalance the "no frills" aspect of the actual flying experience.

As you can see from the examples, with packaged goods it is very easy to move from attribute to benefit. Retail and service companies are a bit more challenging, because their business attributes don't always make for compelling advertising benefits. The challenge is to balance what may be more compelling copy with what is the greatest attribute.

The most challenging area in which to derive customer benefits from business attributes is in the business-to-business area. Let's take a look at the example of Waste Management. Picking up trash and putting it in a landfill isn't exactly the most glamorous job, but it certainly is a necessity of life. While Waste Management does pick up residential trash, the firm's main revenue generators are commercial trash collection and landfill management. The company is also the largest recycling company in North America. Imagine for a moment that you are the head of Ford Motor Company's plants. You have some pretty nasty and toxic waste to dispose of and because you are a publicly traded company, you have significant shareholder responsibility for making sure that all waste is properly disposed of. You would likely be very happy to find a company that would ensure all the waste you disposed of was in compliance with government regulations. You might also be able to show you were progressive by recycling certain materials, and you could guarantee that all the waste was dealt with in a similar manner regardless of where the assembly plant is located in North America. While waste disposal might not be something that is top-of-mind, for some businesspeople it is a huge issue and a potential liability.

While compliance might be the most compelling benefit to a large corporation, from a communication perspective, you may choose to feature innovation. Most large companies want to associate with other innovative, large companies. Rather than scare them with a compliance-warning message, you may want to communicate how innovative you are and how innovative that makes them by association.

Functional benefits involve taking those business attributes and looking at them from a consumer standpoint. It is what the attribute does for the consumer or customer that makes the difference. One of the difficult tasks for the account planner is to ferret out the most compelling benefits that can be communicated effectively. The greatest business attribute may or may not be the most compelling possible communication.

Many brands have been created by relentlessly advertising their functional benefits. However, there comes a time for some brands when promoting just a functional benefit may not be a real point of difference. At that time, you need to look further than a functional benefit to differentiate your brand. You need to look to the emotional benefit.

Emotional Benefits

A great old pretelevision copywriting textbook sums up emotional versus functional benefits in very common-sense terms. In his 1936 book *How to Write Advertising,* author Kenneth Goode talks about "selling the effect" copy. His example at that period was Simmons mattresses. Simmons was the leader in mattress sales and touted a very comfortable mattress. As the category leader, Simmons could consider selling the effect of a good night's sleep, rather than stressing only the functional benefit of a comfy mattress.

In this case, Goode outlines the "sell the effect-of-the-effect" copy. In the Simmons example, he goes on to say that instead of selling the mattress or even "better sleep," Simmons could go even further in its advertising claims. The effect of getting a good night's sleep could lead to better health or even personal success. In essence, all of these "effects of the effect" encompass a handy way to think about an emotional benefit.

If a functional benefit is a product-performance benefit, then the emotional benefit is the personal-performance benefit. It is what the product does for that person's life.

Another great example of this is selling razor blades. Over the years, razor blades have gotten more sophisticated, but the product itself is designed to give a close shave. So, what does having a close shave mean to a man? It might mean looking one's best, which could be the differentiating factor in getting a great job, or getting a good-looking woman. Who thought a simple razor blade could evoke such emotions? As an account planner, it is your job to help the client and the creative teams see the "effect of the effect." It is important to understand how a brand, service, or company fits into the consumer's life.

Plus or Minus Emotions

One way to think about emotional benefits is that the brand can have one of two effects on a person's life. It can add a positive or it can remove a negative. For every advertised item, you can develop this train of thought. Do I add a positive experience to the consumers' lives or do I spare them from a negative experience? Some advertising practitioners refer to these differences as positive appeals and negative appeals.

In the preceding razor example, you can add to a man's life by making him look better. By looking better, he feels better about himself, which in turn gives him more confidence. If a man is confident about himself, he is more likely to get a better job or the woman of his dreams. You get the idea. It is continuing to ask what the product does for the consumer.

Table 5.3 shows some of the emotions that can add a positive or remove a negative experience. As you look at this list, you can think of products that capitalize on one side of the equation or the other. For example, all deodorants certainly remove a negative. Having body odor is a pretty disgusting thing. So, while the functional benefit of a deodorant is to mask the body's odor, the emotional benefit is to make sure that people don't turn up their noses when they get close to you.

As you look at the list of positive and negative experiences, the one area that is a classic for advertising is the area of sensory pleasures. This can be removing a negative sensory experience, such as body odor, or adding a sensory experience, such as making your clothes smell fresh after they are washed. The senses are a good place to start when identifying emotions that can be released. Consumers want positive experiences, whether in taste,

Table 5.3

Emotional Benefit

Add a positive experience	Remove a negative experience

Through sensory pleasures:
  Smell
  Taste
  Sight
  Sound
  Tactile
	Removal of negative sensory experience:
	  Body odor
	  Loud noises
	  Sweaty hands

Elevating personal importance:
  Pride
  Recognition
  Gratitude
	Relief from negative aspects of the person:
	  Ridiculed
	  Loathed
	  Disgusting

Through excitement, amusement, or ecstasy	Through removal of fear, sadness, anger, or surprise

sound, sight, or tactile feelings. This is why advertising professionals spend countless hours crafting advertising messages incorporating many of these sensory elements into the presentation.

Carrying forward our previous examples of Hunt's, Home Depot, Southwest Airlines, and Waste Management, let's see what emotional benefits they might unlock.

In the case of Hunt's, there are obviously sensory benefits that can be tapped into. The taste of a great meal is a pretty obvious one for Hunt's and, for that matter, all food brands. This is why most food advertising has what is called a "bite and smile" aspect to the creative execution. You want to show the emotional benefit of people enjoying the great taste of your food products. Digging a bit deeper than just the sensory emotions, you could make the case that a parent feels gratified because they are serving a meal that their family loves. This makes that parent feel pretty good. So, you may be adding some self-esteem to the mix.

In the case of Home Depot, the consumer feels pride in a job well done. It is an empowering feeling to knock out a home improvement project yourself instead of hiring a professional to do it. Those expert salespeople give the consumer more than just the materials and instruction to accomplish the task; they give him or her some personal power. Now think about the theme line of their advertising campaign, "You can do it. We can help." It is encouraging the consumer to feel pride in getting the job done.

Southwest Airlines is a reliable, inexpensive airline. On an emotional

Table 5.4

Functional Benefits to Emotional Benefits

Brand	Functional benefit	Emotional benefit
Hunt's	Vine-ripened, freshest-tasting tomatoes	Smell and taste of a great meal
		Feel good about serving the best to your family
Home Depot	Expert advice of former tradesmen	Pride in doing your own improve-ment project
Southwest Airlines	Reliable, inexpensive travel	Freedom to travel whenever you want
Waste Management	All waste will be in government compliance	No surprises in taking care of my needs

level, this is a freeing experience. It gives you the freedom to travel. By removing the barriers of cost, time, and delays, there is an emotional benefit of being able to control your own destiny in travel. It is a release of the travel burden. Southwest Airlines' advertising slogan "You are now free to move about the country," taps into this emotional benefit.

For Waste Management, the functional benefit of ensuring all your waste is dealt with in a responsible manner means that there are no surprises for you. It can be a relief to know you don't have to worry about something that could be a huge issue, depending on your business. Waste Management advertising points to this emotional benefit in the slogan "From everyday collection to environmental protection. Think Green. Think Waste Management." The advertising is selling the good stewards of the business, removing a huge potential negative from one's business life.

Emotional benefits are also called higher-order benefits. The reason to focus on emotional benefits is because a functional benefit may not be unique or compelling (see Table 5.4). If every razor blade gives a smooth, clean shave, then you need to move to a higher-order benefit to help differentiate your brand. In a world of parity products, it is typically the brand that arrives at the emotional benefit first that wins in the marketplace. As you could see from our previous examples, all of these category leaders have some expression of an emotional benefit in their advertising.

If you can capture the emotional benefit of the brand and can reflect it compellingly in the advertising, then you have a powerful tool. Consumers may try your product based on a product feature or functional benefit. However, consumers will bond with you and be much less likely to switch brands if they can connect with you on an emotional level.

Benefit Laddering

Now it is time to put it all together. You understand your product's attributes and how they benefit the consumer both functionally and emotionally. You have a firm grasp on your target customers and what makes them tick. One way to pull all this information together is through an exercise called benefit laddering.

Figure 5.1 details a benefit ladder for Tide laundry detergent. As you can see, the base of the ladder is a description of the target market. In this case, it is women with families who have a penchant for getting their clothes dirty. The product, Tide, has some unique attributes making it a great product. It has special formulas that get clothes clean and leaves them without soap residue, which can break down the fibers. The benefit is it gets clothes clean and makes them last longer than other detergents. So how does this help the target customer? It taps into her cost-conscious head. She feels smart, even if she spent a little more on Tide, because she doesn't have to buy clothes as often since they stay looking new longer. In this case, Tide may help the mother be a hero in a household where budgets are tight.

You can and should perform this exercise for any company with which you are working. There can be more than one functional and emotional benefit, so just experiment. The foundation of the exercise is the target market. In this case, the Tide consumer is very cost-conscious, so that is a driving force in solving her consumer problem. Once you have the consumer, then you fill in the product attributes. From there you derive the functional benefit and "ladder up" into the emotional benefits.

The benefit laddering exercise is a good one to conduct with company managers, to encourage them to continue to explore the higher-order benefits of the products or services they are marketing. It is also a common exercise that is conducted in qualitative research. Researchers will ask consumers, either in focus groups or one-on-one settings, to describe why they buy a product and then to ladder up into increasingly emotional benefits. For example, the majority of mothers are going to say they buy Tide because it gets their clothes clean and makes them last longer. If possible, most people will give a rational answer to the question. However, a good qualitative researcher can begin to ask questions

Figure 5.1   **Benefit Ladder: Tide Example**

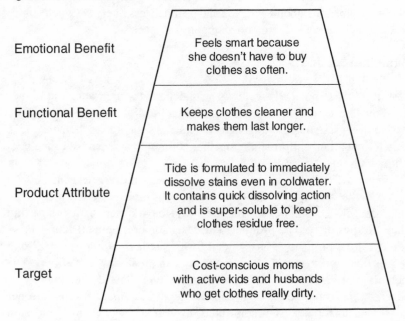

Emotional Benefit — Feels smart because she doesn't have to buy clothes as often.

Functional Benefit — Keeps clothes cleaner and makes them last longer.

Product Attribute — Tide is formulated to immediately dissolve stains even in coldwater. It contains quick dissolving action and is super-soluble to keep clothes residue free.

Target — Cost-conscious moms with active kids and husbands who get clothes really dirty.

such as, "So, how does that help you?" or "How does that make you feel? Does your husband notice it?" With a deeper line of questioning, researchers can help unlock some of the emotional benefits that are contained in most products.

Benefit Matrix

Now we are going to throw you a curveball. We have spent this chapter working on how you move from a product attribute to a consumer benefit to an emotional benefit. This logic train is good, but the problem is that nearly all products, goods, and services have multiple benefits. What makes this process even more difficult is that different target markets can have totally different motivations for buying the same product. For example, a Saturn automobile is a great first car. Young drivers who are attracted to it find it sporty, easy to handle, and accepted by their peers as being cool. Parents, who may be paying for the car or the insurance or both, might be attracted to it because it is affordable and durable. It is the same car, but there are two very different motivations explaining why Saturn might be a good choice.

Table 5.5

Benefit Matrix: Orville Redenbacher Gourmet Popcorn

	Health-conscious moms	
Target market	with tweens and teenage kids	Fun-loving tweens and girls
Product attribute	Orville Redenbacher Gourmet Popcorn is made with top 20% corn, which pops lighter and fluffier, with fewer unpopped kernels than competition. Popcorn is a good source of dietary fiber.	
Consumer benefit	A healthy alternative to chips plus best-quality popcorn that I deserve.	Easy to make and always tastes great. I can share with my friends.
Emotional benefit	I don't feel guilty about indulging on a snack.	Orville makes parties and time with friends more fun.

How do we deal with this disparity in rolling up our benefit ladder? After doing the laddering exercise, it is also wise to build a benefit matrix. A benefit matrix can be used to account for differing target markets. You may have a benefit matrix containing different demographic groups, differing mindsets, or differing behaviors. Regardless of the situation, you can use the benefit matrix to capture these differences.

Look at the sample benefit matrix for Orville Redenbacher popcorn (see Table 5.5). The two target markets are moms and tween girls (ages 8–12). Unlike the benefit laddering, where the target market is the foundation of the ladder, here you have different columns for various target markets. The one row remaining constant in the matrix contains the product attributes of the brand in question. In this case, Orville Redenbacher popcorn has some unique attributes in how it is made, making it the leading popcorn brand.

As you can see, while the product attributes are the same, these two consumer groups have different reasons for using the product. For the mom, the popcorn brand taps into her need to feed her kids healthy snacks. She would much rather have her kids eat popcorn than chips or other items, so she doesn't feel guilty about letting her kids munch a bunch of popcorn. Tween girls, on the other hand, couldn't care less about eating healthy, but they do care about what their friends think of them, particularly when they are hosting sleepovers. For this group, Orville Redenbacher does a couple of things. First, it is a snack they can make themselves, so they feel empowered. Second, it is fun and makes sharing a good time. It is a social event for a group that may sometimes have social phobias.

Summary

Defining the benefit is one of the most crucial aspects of being an account planner. To get to the heart of the benefit, it is important to understand that any brand, service, or company is devoted to building unique attributes. These attributes are the cornerstone of their businesses. However, you can add a tremendous amount of value to the company by evaluating the brand from a consumer perspective. Determining the consumer benefits, both functionally and emotionally, is a crucial task to the marketing and advertising process. Unless you focus your communication on a relevant and compelling benefit, it will not likely help increase your brand's sales. You should challenge the brand to "ladder up" its benefits from functional to emotional. Just like climbing Jacob's ladder, the first brand to reach the top of the emotional ladder usually wins the race.

Review Questions

1. What are the differences between attributes and benefits? How do attributes help an advertiser? How to benefits help an advertiser?
2. What kinds of products and services make use of sensory attributes?
3. What are possible attributes for automobiles, retail stores, liquid cleansers, television sets, and pest control services?
4. Now, what are possible benefits for each of the categories mentioned in the previous question?

Discussion Questions

1. Analyze the higher order on the benefit ladder. What are the advantages of the higher positions? What are the disadvantages?
2. Analyze the functional, emotional, and sensory characteristics of products and services. What are the advantages of each? What are the disadvantages?

Exercises

1. Collect several brands of cleaning products, such as Lysol, Pine Sol, Mr. Clean, Comet, and others. Analyze the attributes of each brand. Then analyze the benefits of each brand.
2. Using the same cleaning products, analyze the functional, emotional, and sensory characteristics of each brand.

CBC Case Study

Use the CBC information from Chapter 1.

1. Analyze the attributes of CBC and each of its major competitors.
2. Now analyze the benefits of CBC and its major competitors as:

   - Functional benefits;
   - Emotional benefits;
   - Sensory benefits.

Additional Sources

Fox, Jeffrey J., and Richard C. Gregory. *The Dollarization Discipline: How Smart Companies Create Customer Value . . . and Profit from It.* New York: Wiley, 2004.

Goode, Kenneth M. *How to Write Advertising.* New York: Longmans, Green and Co., 1936.

Hill, Dan. *Body of Truth: Leveraging What Consumers Can't or Won't Say.* New York: Wiley, 2003.

Reynolds, Thomas J., and Jerry C. Olson. *Understanding Consumer Decision Making: A Means-End Approach to Marketing and Advertising Strategy.* Mahwah, NJ; London: Lawrence Erlbaum, 2000.

Zaltman, Gerald. *How Customers Think: Essential Insights into the Mind of the Market.* Boston, MA: Harvard Business School Press, 2003.

Chapter 6
Brand Personality

One of the most powerful traits any brand or company has is its personality. Just about every company takes on some sort of personality traits, just as individuals do. Brands or companies can be playful, sophisticated, down home, or even sexy. Some brands have a personality by default and others capitalize on their personality just like they would in distinguishing a business attribute.

As an account planner, your role is to help a company or brand recognize the importance of cultivating its personality. It can be a very powerful marketing tool both inside and outside a company. Defining the brand's personality is also a crucial aspect of developing communications for the brand. Before advertising is conceived and created, copywriters and art directors must understand the brand's personality. It is no different than an actor understanding the character for a role in a play.

Why Brand Personality Is Important

Brand personality is simply the human character attributes of the brand. By this, we mean that if you were describing the brand or company as a person, what are the adjectives you would use to describe it? Some companies have very clear and calculated personalities, while others are very muddled.

Perhaps the question many corporate executives ask is, "Does it really matter?" In Chapter 5, we discussed how much effort goes into determining the most appropriate or compelling benefit for your target market. Companies and brands are very focused on building unique business attributes that no one else has. As a result, a company's brand personality can get the short end of the stick. Many company executives believe the personality is some sort of "touchy-feely" exercise that may not have much business merit.

But as the account planner you know that having a strong brand personality can be a very strong differentiator. It can be more enduring than a functional benefit. It can be as strong as zeroing in on an emotional benefit. This is particularly true in categories where it is difficult to gain a compelling functional benefit. Examples of these commodity categories are banking, shipping, temporary personnel services, and gas stations. Let's face it: Don't you just go to the bank that is most convenient? When is the last time you have bonded with a gas station? Or can you really tell one "temp" service from another? From a functional benefit standpoint, all these categories are extremely similar. Where a brand can stand out is in the area of brand personality.

One such example was in the late 1990s in the banking industry in Texas. Before being acquired by Washington Mutual in the 2001, Bank United had a remarkable run in market share and deposit growth in the state. The bank attributed much of its success to its very unbank-like marketing position and advertising campaign. Unlike at stately banks, Bank United employees wore jeans and t-shirts. They introduced bold products like "Free checking for life." Their advertising was very different as well. To set the bank apart, the advertising firm FogartyKleinMonroe recommended the bank move from the Bank United name to Bank U in its advertising. In essence, it helped create a nickname for the bank. It then adopted a slogan, "Thank you, Bank U." The bank advertisements also used two former Saturday Night Live personalities who became "consumer commandos." Their mission was to rid the world of staid banking practices and to move consumers to Bank U. The Bank's growth and subsequent large premium selling price to Washington Mutual was accomplished by developing a brand personality that transcended the organization.

There are also many categories that are built with brand personality as the lead ingredient. All fashion categories, such as clothing, perfume, and cosmetics, are largely driven by personality. Leisure products such as golf and tennis take on the personalities of the athletes endorsing them. Nike has built a huge business on personality-driven athletic performance shoes. Motorcycles, fishing gear, sports franchises, and all other leisure and entertainment categories have huge personality components as their main point of difference. Building a strong brand personality can have a big financial payoff.

Personality Is Not Advertising Tonality

Many people confuse a brand personality with the tone of the advertising. Many advertising executives have heard corporation chiefs ask them to create a personality for their company through advertising. While advertising can do a lot to magnify or expand a brand's personality, it is not a substitute for it.

For example, there is the down-home expression, "You can put a dress on a pig but it's still a pig." This is exactly the challenge advertising firms face when dealing with brand personality. If the consumer experience is that the personality of the brand is serious, no amount of "hype" or dancing chickens will likely persuade them to perceive it as fun. The company would have to make a true effort to change its ways and "lighten up."

The earlier example of Bank United is a classic case in brand personality aligning with advertising tonality. The bank rallied behind its advertising campaign. The firm was already trying to be unbank-like but then turned it up a notch. The employees changed the way they answered the telephone. They had small office parties. They celebrated their customers' successes. Unless the brand personality and the advertising tonality are in sync, you are likely to have a bit of disconnect.

A brand personality is very human and must have some sort of resonance with the brand. It can't be the flavor of the week. It is as much a strategic asset as a functional benefit. Just as Bank United did, many service organizations rely heavily on personality as their distinguishing characteristic.

Having said this, are you locked into certain type of advertising to convince customers that your brand is serious? The answer is, of course not. Just as a character in a story has different emotions, so does your company or brand. While General Motors is certainly an American icon, it has updated its looks to match its persona. Its Chevrolet truck advertising theme, "Like a Rock," sung to the old Detroit singer Bob Seeger's tune, drives a hard-rocking commercial. Chevrolet's brand personality roots are certainly heartland-oriented and this song plays off that fact. It isn't mom and apple pie, but it is heartland America.

Brand personality is a more central characteristic of the company or product than advertising tonality. Advertising executions can come and go but the brand personality and its characteristics should remain steady.

Defining a Brand's Personality

There are a number of schemes for defining a brand's personality. Various research companies and advertising agencies have their own proprietary methods for defining and profiling a brand's personality. One of the classic published analyses on the topic comes from David Aaker's book, *Building Strong Brands,* where he outlines a brand personality scale categorizing brands into five overall personalities. He dubs these as the "Big 5 Personalities." The five groups are: sincerity, excitement, competence, sophistication, and ruggedness.

Aaker found that, in extensive research with a thousand respondents who rated sixty brands using 114 different personality traits, the Big 5 explained 93 percent of all observed differences between these brands. This result

Table 6.1

A Brand Personality Scale (BPS): The Big 5

Sincerity (Campbell's, Hallmark, Kodak)
- Down-to-Earth: family-oriented, small-town, conventional, blue-collar, all-American
- Honest: sincere, real, ethical, thoughtful, caring
- Wholesome: original, genuine, ageless, classic, old-fashioned
- Cheerful: sentimental, friendly, warm, happy

Excitement (Porsche, Absolute, Benetton)
- Daring: trendy, exciting, off-beat, flashy, provocative
- Spirited: cool, young, lively, outgoing, adventurous
- Imaginative: unique, humorous, surprising, artistic, fun
- Up-to-date: independent, contemporary, innovative, aggressive

Competence (AMEX, CNN, IBM)
- Reliable: hardworking, secure, efficient, trustworthy, careful
- Intelligent: technical, corporate, serious
- Successful: leader, confident, influential

Sophistication (Lexus, Mercedes, Revlon)
- Upper class: glamorous, good-looking, pretentious, sophisticated
- Charming: feminine, smooth, sexy, gentle

Ruggedness (Levi's, Marlboro, Nike)
- Outdoorsy: masculine, western, active, athletic
- Tough: rugged, strong, no-nonsense

either says that it is a great study or that most brands are pretty similar. Actually, this is a very strong study and should be considered as an important tool for any account planner.

As you look at the Big 5 Personality groups, you will see subgroups and subgroups to the subgroups (see Table 6.1). For example, under the sincerity umbrella, there are down-to-earth, honest, wholesome, and cheerful subgroups. These are directions toward which a brand in the sincerity arena can migrate. Even within the cheerful subgroup, it is further refined to finer differences: sentimental, friendly, warm, and happy. The point of this subgrouping is to dimensionalize each personality trait.

This analysis is important either in gaining some distance from another brand or to reposition your brand into a more favorable light. Wal-Mart is certainly in the sincerity category but it falls in the down-to-earth subgroup.

Figure 6.1   **Big 5 Personality Linkage: McDonald's**

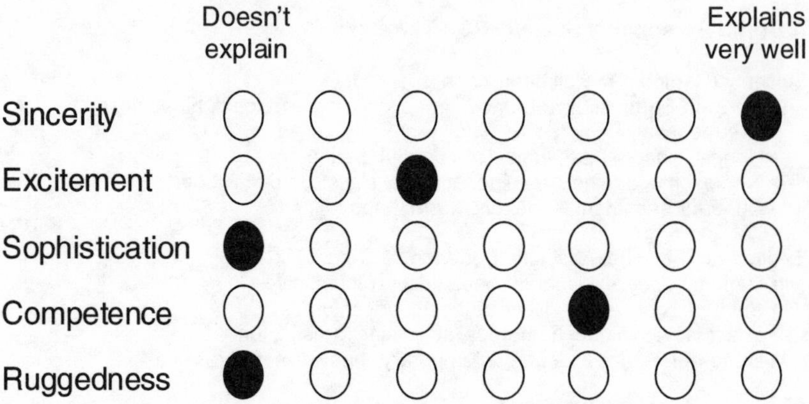

	Doesn't explain						Explains very well
Sincerity	○	○	○	○	○	○	●
Excitement	○	○	●	○	○	○	○
Sophistication	●	○	○	○	○	○	○
Competence	○	○	○	○	●	○	○
Ruggedness	●	○	○	○	○	○	○

You could make the case that Wal-Mart once had a very small-town personality and feel. As the company has gotten larger, it has seemingly moved away from the small-town feel to a more family-oriented image. The stores are still down-to-earth but the subtle personality traits of the brand have likely slightly changed over time.

As you assess a brand, remember that, just like a person, no one brand fits neatly into these five categories. You are likely to have a dominant and a less-dominant personality trait. For example, a brand like McDonald's is very high in the sincerity category. Ronald McDonald is all about sincerity; however, the McDonald's company and brand also have a competence air about them. McDonald's is an operational machine. It is extremely strong on operational efficiency ranging from how to make the food to how to keep the restaurants clean. Or take a brand like BMW. BMW would be high in the excitement category as well as in the sophistication category.

You can use the brand personality scale to measure the degree to which the personality categories and traits reflect the brand. You can also compare one brand to another to see where you might be able to exploit some differences. Sometimes it is as important to understand what your brand isn't as much as what it is.

Figure 6.1 illustrates how you can apply a seven-point scale to each of the brand-personality categories. The example reflects McDonald's, which has a good sincerity association, but not sophistication or ruggedness. As you direct advertising executions, you wouldn't want to see Ronald

McDonald dressed like James Bond or getting into a knife fight. That would be a bit out of character for the brand. The biggest area of opportunity for the brand is to continue to dial up the excitement level of the brand. While McDonald's may not be exciting to teens or adults, it certainly is exciting to young children. There is a component of family excitement for the brand.

Challenging the Category Personality

Most people have a feeling about any product category that is available in the marketplace. You may think jewelry is sophisticated or exciting. You likely would want your electricity provider to be reliable. You probably feel your stockbroker should be savvy and serious with your money.

Every product category has a personality profile. It is an expectation when you are purchasing a particular good or service. For the most part, the category leader takes on the overall personality of the category. In Table 6.2, we have listed four different categories and a category leader in each. While their brand personalities are different, they do follow a similar pattern. Most people expect their banks to be pretty serious. After all, it is your money; you don't want some silly person handling your money, do you? Yet, in our example of Bank United, the company used this understanding to its advantage and went against the banking stereotype.

In fact, as you eye each of these categories, you may see another pattern emerge. Going against the expected personality of a category could yield very good results. Apple Computer is the anti-IBM. While IBM is very corporate, Apple doesn't take itself too seriously and is very fun. Apple went against the category and its leader to carve out an interesting business and personality niche for itself.

In the cosmetics arena, the majority of brands carry some level of sophistication, while some brands are more contemporary than others (e.g., Estée Lauder vs. Clinique), but for the most part cosmetics play to women's aspirational desires. Ironically, Mary Kay Cosmetics built a business by going against the grain in nearly every aspect of cosmetics. Mary Kay is sold in the home by a neighbor, the packages are plain, and the representatives are selling natural products. The brand is about as "down-home" as you can get in a category that can be very pretentious.

Even in the motorcycle area, there are contrasts among some of the major brands. You expect a motorcycle to be rugged. Harley Davidson has capitalized on this fact by having more white-collar "weekend warriors" riding their motorcycles than Hell's Angels members. Contrast this approach

Table 6.2

Personality: Category-Positioning Exercise

Category	Expected personality	Category leader	Personality	Opposite personality
Cosmetics	Sophistication	Clinique	Sophistication	Down home
Computers	Corporate	IBM	Corporate	Fun
Motorcycles	Rugged	Harley Davidson	Rugged	Gentle
Banking	Serious	Bank of America	Serious	Silly

with that of Honda, which presents a gentler image of getting back to nature with the motorcycle.

Personality can be a real differentiator and it can be used strategically to look at how to attack a category, not only from an advertising or brand perspective but from a business perspective as well.

How to Define Brand Personality

There are a lot of research techniques for helping define a brand personality. One of the typical methods used to help sort out one brand's personality from another is through a word-association test.

In a word-association test, a respondent is asked to assign words that best fit the brand. This can be done by free association, where a respondent rattles off words first coming to mind that might describe a brand (known in the business as "top-of-head" recognition), or through a written exercise, where the researcher may give the respondent a choice of words to assign or associate with the brand.

Look at the example of a portion of a word-association test where respondents were asked to use a semantic-differential scale to associate beer brands. In this case, you ask the respondent to classify a brand from one extreme to another to assess the association. The example before you shows the differences between Budweiser and Corona beer. You can see that the two beers have very different associations.

Budweiser is heavily associated with being masculine, blue-collar, old-fashioned, real, and plain. On the other hand, Corona is a bit more feminine, contemporary, and sexy. Both brands lie somewhere between humorous and serious (see Figure 6.4).

Figure 6.4 **Personality Profile: Two-Brand Comparison—Budweiser Versus Corona**

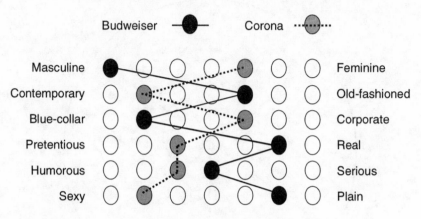

Depending upon the brand and the intent of the exercise, you can add as many pairs of descriptors as you feel necessary to get a read on the brand's personality association.

There are other qualitative techniques commonly used to round out a brand's personality profile. One such technique is a picture sort, where consumers look at a variety of pictures and pick the ones that best fit the brand. Many researchers use a range of pictures of drinks, cars, shoes, or houses to determine the associations. Other researchers ask consumers to bring in their own pictures that they feel represent the brand. From there, the researcher will ask probing questions to get at the emotions the consumer might associate with the brand.

Other popular associations are with famous people or sports celebrities. You can ask a consumer, "If this brand were a celebrity who would it be?" Any range of items that can demonstrate a personality or emotional range is fair game. It is important to use the same technique to gain some sort of validation and base of experience. All of these methods are projection techniques allowing consumers to stretch their minds when they are discussing your brand.

One last method to discuss is a sensory method. You may want to ask the consumer to discuss a brand using each of the senses. For example, you could ask the consumer to listen to a variety of music that might describe the brand. You may have various smells cued up to cause a consumer to react. Or you might even have various textures that consumers could touch to describe the brand. All of these methods, when put together, can help draw out a brand story or personality.

Figure 6.5 **Sample for a Possible Brand Story**

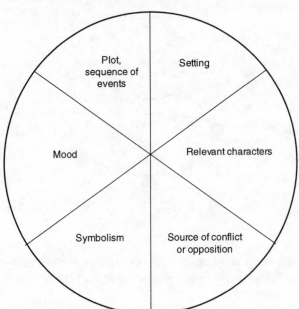

Developing a Brand Story

The majority of marketing and advertising research is very much on the informational side of the ledger. This is why developing the brand personality is so important. It helps to humanize the brand. For advertising creative directors, knowing the brand personality is one step in understanding how best to link the brand's values with the values that humans desire. When brand values connect on an emotional level, you can have a much stronger bond than just through a functional benefit.

Personality, in and of itself, is not the stopping point for creative exploration. Advertising that gives the product drama is the most compelling. To give the product some drama, you must understand the brand's story. Just like Shakespeare's play *Hamlet*, a brand is made up of story ingredients. A story typically includes a lead character, a setting, other characters, a source of conflict or opposition, symbolism, mood, and some plot or sequence of events (see Figure 6.5).

Like a novelist creating a story, an account planner looks for the inherent drama in the product. However, the planner is looking for drama in a different vein than a novelist. Here are the areas an account planner or a qualitative researcher probes:

1. Setting: Where is the product most enjoyed?
2. Characters: What role does it play in relationships between people?
3. Opposition: What are the relevant conflicts or oppositions?
4. Symbols: What aspects of people's experience of the product suggest symbols or metaphors?
5. Mood: How do people feel when using the product?
6. Plot: What role does it play in some sequence of events?

In each of these areas that comprise a story, we are looking for memory cures or what novelist Cecilia Bartholomew calls "irrelevancies." Irrelevancies are those seemingly unimportant bits and pieces of information of daily life, giving it some emotional texture. For example, sitting in your pajamas while sipping coffee and reading the morning paper is a string of irrelevancies. However, if you were working on advertising for Folger's brand coffee, those irrelevancies might make for a compelling coffee story or bring the brand's personality to life. Let's face it: Jerry Seinfeld has made a great comedic career out of bringing irrelevancies to life. It is the account planner's job to investigate brands at this level to determine whether there are social links that can be exploited by the brand.

There are a number of ways to get after the brand's story. One method is to ask consumers to write their own brand story. By allowing consumers to write a story, you will often free them to give you a much deeper sense of the brand's personality and linkage to real-life events. When you have ten individual stories, you can then edit them into a single story for the brand, while also learning the similarities among the things the majority of the consumers associate with your brand.

The more traditional way to get at the brand's story is to do ethnographic research. Ethnographic research is when a researcher actually spends time with the brand users or their families when they are using the product. For example, they might go home with a mother and watch her prepare the family meal and observe the interaction amid the family members during the meal. After observing a series of consumer respondents, the ethnographic researcher will then write her observations and resulting brand story.

Figure 6.6 illustrates an example of a brand story for Kool-Aid from the 1988 article by Jeffrey Durgee, "Understanding Brand Personality." Through

Figure 6.6   **Story Lines for the Kool-Aid Brand Story**

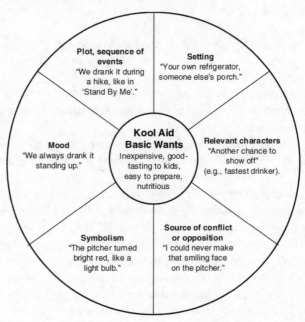

Source: Jeffrey Durgee, "Understanding Brand Personality," *The Journal of Consumer Marketing* 5, no. 3 (1988). Reprinted with permission.

qualitative research techniques, consumers were asked to fill in the story line for the Kool-Aid brand.

As you can see from this example, there is a lot of symbolism and many metaphors used when discussing this brand. The ice-cold pitcher full of Kool-Aid itself has become an icon for the brand. The pitcher magically turning colors is a transforming experience. The brand is also very active in people's minds; they think of drinking Kool-Aid while playing tennis, camping out, or hiking. It is also a social drink, whether at home or somewhere else.

As you can see, the story-telling technique adds tremendous texture to the brand personality. It is a critical aspect of taking the brand personality to the next level. As an account planner, you will want to use traditional research, such as word association and other tests, to draw out the brand's personality. Then you should add texture to the outline of this personality profile through story-telling explorations.

Brand personality is an important ingredient for any brand or company. It can be a powerful competitive advantage and it is one of the key elements for creating compelling advertising.

Review Questions

1. Do products and services really have personalities?
2. Why might personalities be preferred to traditional product or service benefits in planning a promotional campaign?
3. Can noncontact and impersonal products and services have personalities? Can an Internet website have a personality?
4. Why are brand personalities important? Is it possible for the personality to be more important than the actual product or service being marketed?

Discussion Questions

1. Identify several banks that operate in your community. Analyze the personalities for each bank. What are the similarities and what are the differences?
2. Using personalities, analyze the differences between United Parcel Service and FedEx.
3. If a product has more commodity characteristics, is there likely to be more or less reliance on the product's personality in the marketing of that product? Why?
4. What kinds of music might be appropriate for advertising: an investment firm, an airline, fast food, a sports car, and military enlistments?

Exercises

1. Select several brands of products and services. Match public figures and their public personalities as possible endorsers for those brands.
2. For the same brands, try to match their brand personalities with their personality profiles.

CBC Case Study

Build on the CBC case from Chapter 1.

1. What brand personality can you identify to aid in the promotion of CBC's products?
2. How can these personalities be utilized in the promotion of CBC's products?

3. Do all of CBC's products necessarily have the same personalities?
4. Develop CBC's personality profile.
5. Finally, develop a brand story for CBC.

Additional Sources

Aaker, David A. *Building Strong Brands*. New York: Free Press, 1996.
Durgee, Jeffery. "Understanding Brand Personality." *The Journal of Consumer Marketing* 5 (Summer 1988): 21–25.
Fog, Klaus. *Storytelling: Branding in Practice*. Berlin; New York: Springer, 2005.
Keller, Kevin Lane. *Building Customer-Based Brand Equity: A Blueprint for Creating Strong Brands*. Cambridge, MA: Marketing Science Institute, 2001.
Moser, Mike. *United We Brand: How to Create a Cohesive Brand That's Seen, Heard and Remembered*. Boston, MA: Harvard Business School Press, 2003.
Shaw, Colin, and John Ivens. *Building Great Customer Experiences*. New York: Palgrave Macmillan, 2004.

Chapter 7
Brand Positioning

If your brand is not positioned in the marketplace correctly, all the hard work to build the attributes that translate into the consumer benefits is for naught. To position the brand, you need to define the company's strengths and weaknesses. You need to know your target market inside and out and you must be able to translate the company's attributes into consumer benefits. You then need to combine all this with the brand's personality or story. All of the material so far in this book culminates in the brand positioning.

As an account planner, it is your role to make sure the brand is properly positioned. If you are working with a packaged-goods manufacturer, you might work with brand management on this task, or you might do this largely on your own with a retail or business-to-business company. Regardless of the situation, you must know the tenets of brand positioning to move the company forward. It is the cornerstone of all marketing and communication efforts.

Classic Brand Positioning

Table 7.1 is a brand positioning statement that originated from Procter & Gamble brand management practices. Most consumer companies use some form of this statement today as their brand positioning statement.

Let's discuss all the elements in the brand positioning statement and how they interact. The first blank to fill in is the target market definition. If you go back to Chapter 4, "Defining the Target Market," you will see that this is where you develop a conceptual target. The target definition of the positioning statement must have more than just a demographic definition. For example, it is not enough to say the target is "moms with kids" for a food brand. You must paint a picture of the motivation of the target market. Is it "choosey moms" or "penny-pinching moms" or "health-conscious moms"? To have a successful brand position, you must help define the need state of the target market. It is from this need state that, we hope, the brand will deliver its benefit.

The second aspect of the brand positioning statement is the frame of

---

Table 7.1

Brand Positioning Statement

To _____, _____ is the brand of
(TARGET MARKET)   (BRAND)

_____   that _____
(COMPETITIVE FRAMEWORK)   (BENEFIT)

because _____
         (REASON WHY)

The brand personality is _____

---

reference. Defining the competitive frame of reference may sound pretty basic, but it does require some careful thought. For example, if we are marketing Brite Smile toothpaste, is our frame of reference all toothpastes or is it only toothpastes that have a whitening agent? Each competitive frame of reference will then have an impact on the subsequent benefit of the brand.

As an account planner, you need to assess the competitive frame of reference in two ways. The first is from the business aspect of the brand. Whom does the brand want to compete against to gain market share? This is a key dynamic on how to position the brand. Second, you need to determine where the vulnerabilities are in the market. However, you need to check this analytical MBA drive with a consumer point of view. It does no good for you to position an Acura automobile against expensive luxury cars if consumers put it in a mid-size sedan set.

Over time, the competitive frame of reference may change or expand as the brand changes and expands. If you are marketing pudding, your initial frame of reference might be all other puddings. Over time, you may want to expand your thinking to all after-dinner desserts. This is especially true if your brand is dominating its immediate niche. To grow, you may need to expand your sights, which could then change the dynamic of the positioning statement.

The third part of the brand positioning statement is the consumer benefit statement. What is the intended customers' "take-away"? You are selling the brand of toothpaste that whitens teeth while it cleans. Or yours is the brand that is the fastest-acting detergent or longest-lasting deodorant. The secret to the brand benefit is to be as precise as possible. You can't be wishy-washy or obtuse in your benefit statement. Clear, matter-of-fact writing is in order here.

Another potential problem with a benefit statement is that it might not be a meaningful point of difference. The benefit should be compelling to the consumer and it should set the brand apart from the competition. It is not enough for toothpaste to whiten teeth or freshen breath. That may indeed be a benefit, but every toothpaste can make that claim; it is the price of entry into the market. The benefit should be so unique that you cannot substitute another brand in the positioning statement. This is a good "sniff" test for your positioning statement. The more commodity-like the brand is, the more difficult the task of developing a meaningful point of difference.

Following the benefit statement comes the "reason (or reasons) why." This section is the support for the benefit. If you have a toothpaste that whitens teeth the best, the reason why may be a new formula combining a bleaching agent with a cleaning agent. The purpose of the "reason why" is to make the benefit believable. Without a firm foundation, the benefit is nothing but an empty promise or puffery. The reason why must be some sort of fact-based information. As an account planner, you need to make sure not only that the facts are there but that these facts can also lead to consumer inspiration.

To consumers, the reason why must be understandable as well as believable. Just because a car comes with a gyroscope that adjusts steering to automatically groove the car on the highway doesn't mean the average consumer will understand it or necessarily care. If the same navigational device is on a space capsule, then a consumer might see that there is a pretty special reason why. All of these blanks in the positioning statement should be very clear and consumer friendly. This is where the account planner can help brand management craft the statement so it not only makes business sense but also makes consumer sense.

The final aspect of the brand positioning statement is the brand personality. As we talked about in the previous chapter, the brand personality has strategic value. Within the framework of a positioning statement, it is important to sum up the characteristics that make the brand unique. For the positioning statement, you can expand the brand personality to include brand character or brand equity elements. For example, the brand personality of McDonald's is wholesomeness, which is personified by Ronald McDonald. Expanding this definition is appropriate if you have an entrenched brand that is well defined.

If you have a new brand, then you are shaping the brand personality. In that case, you may want to list personality words that epitomize the brand and add a celebrity or some sort of personification for the brand if there is someone who offers a strong representation.

Competitive Brand Positioning Matrix

Now that you have done the brand positioning exercise, it is time to evaluate it within a competitive framework. Although you should have taken into account the competition in the positioning statement itself, sometimes it doesn't become meaningful until you put each competitor side by side with your brand and with your position.

One way to assess the brand's position and to make sure it is crystal clear is to develop a brand positioning matrix where you put your brand in with the competition. Table 7.2 is a brand positioning template that can be used for this task.

Once you and your colleagues have assessed the relationships from this brand personality matrix, you can begin to judge the most compelling position in the marketplace. It might not be your brand; if not, then you may want to step back and see where you might strengthen your brand's positioning vis-à-vis the competition.

This is a great tool with which to play "what if" games with your brand's positioning. You may want to change the target audience or the need state to determine how that action could impact the brand's benefits. This is a particularly useful ploy if a competitor has a stronghold on a certain target segment and you want to crack it. For example, Franco-American's SpaghettiO's were the clear kids' favorite for canned pasta. The vulnerability for SpaghettiO's was as much in the personality as the actual product itself. It was very kidlike and silly. Chef Boyardee painted the picture of its brand as being "beefy" or much more "big-kid oriented" rather than the "little kid" orientation of Franco. This is a classic case of positioning differentiation.

Owning Conceptual Space

Brand positioning and the positioning matrix are very much the stuff of packaged-goods marketing. All packaged-goods manufacturers use some variation of these tools in their marketing tool kits. Packaged-goods marketing is very process-driven, using methods that have been around for some time.

While you can apply some of the methods of packaged-goods marketing to other categories, sometimes that is a bit of a forced fit. It is like putting those size 8 shoes on a size 10 foot; it can be done, but it is a painful process. When you are working with retailers, service companies, or even business-to-business marketers, you should introduce the idea of owning conceptual space.

Table 7.2

Brand Positioning Matrix

Brand/product	Target definition (demographic usage)	Target market (including need state)	Competitive set	Benefit	Reason why	Brand personality
Your brand						
Competition 1						
Competition 2						
Competition 3						

Conceptual space sounds like a mystical thing but it is a simple equation. Conceptual space is usually made up of owning a compelling consumer benefit and also owning a personality trait. When you combine these
two elements, you can carve out a niche in the marketplace. When you look
at conceptual space, you might ask these basic questions:

1. What does the customer want in this category?
2. What companies are strongly associated with these customers'
   wants?
3. Is there a space in these wants that isn't currently being strongly
   occupied?
4. Can we occupy that space in a tangible and credible manner?
5. Do any of our competitors have strong and distinguished marketing programs?
6. What personality attributes are most compelling to the customer?
7. How is our personality aligned with the customer and our competition?

For example, let's take a look at the grocery store marketplace in Houston, Texas. Claiming some conceptual space in the grocery market can be a
daunting task. The consumer benefits for the category are good service and
low price, with specifics such as variety of merchandise and fresh produce
as key ingredients in a consumer's decision to select a grocery store. One
way to elevate this landscape is to develop a conceptual space matrix. This
is exactly what a local Houston grocery chain, Randall's, did to carve out a
significant niche in the market (see Figure 7.1).

In this case, Randall's viewed the marketplace in two ways. The first
was in the dimensions of service from high-touch to low-touch. The second
was in advertising appeals of the grocery chains on the other axis from
emotional to rational. Randall's found most of the grocers occupied the
low-touch and rational-appeal quadrant. The two major national chains,
Kroger and Albertson's, had traditional approaches to the market with nothing special in terms of service and traditional price/item advertising. HEB
Pantry stores were smaller in format than the national chains; HEB Pantry
had an aggressive price campaign to go along with its no-frills and no-
service concept. This was a highly rational appeal built on price. Wal-Mart
was not known for service but was known for low price; its advertising
campaign was more people-oriented but not highly emotional.

Randall's attacked the marketplace both from the service angle on
the business side and from the emotional perspective on the communi-

Figure 7.1 **Houston Grocery Market**

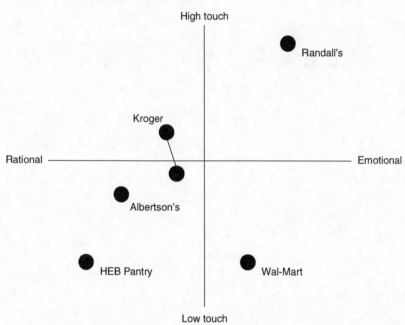

cations side. Randall's had a very high service level with personal touches: from carry-out for the groceries to setting up special parking spots for expectant mothers to calling customers with their pharmacy orders. All these actions were very high-touch. To capture the emotional high ground in communications, the stores used a highly memorable jingle that was built around a theme, "It is not how much we carry but how much we care." By capturing the conceptual space of "caring service," Randall's carved out a solid niche in a very competitive marketplace.

Perhaps the most difficult area in which to own conceptual space is in the business-to-business area. However, Intel semiconductors did just that with its famous "Intel inside" campaign. While other semiconductor manufacturers were fighting to develop the next fastest chip, Intel seized the high ground in the category with reliability as the key business ownership, combined with a fun personality. They took what was a commodity category and made it their category.

Not every business-to-business category can afford to advertise on the scale of Intel. But you can still own conceptual space without spending

Figure 7.2   **Business-to-Business Decision Matrix**

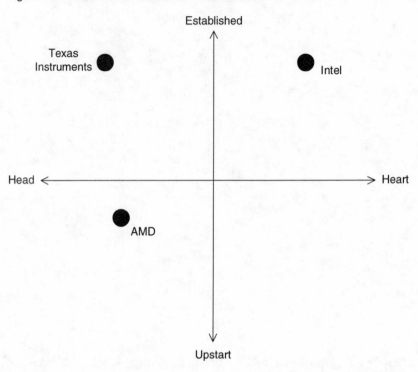

hundreds of millions of dollars on network television. Most business-to-business marketers are either "strivers" or "arrivers." Arrivers are the large, well-established companies in the category. Usually, they have size and proven methods for doing business. They are a safe choice. Strivers, on the other hand, are the upstarts in the category. They usually have new methods that might be more advanced than the arrivers but perhaps not as proven, or they may be more of a boutique and offer faster or better service. While price certainly factors into any equation, it is not usually a killer attribute for business-to-business companies.

Just as for retail or services, you can set up a matrix for business-to-business brands (see Figure 7.2). One method to begin with is to look at how established a business is on one axis and how it markets itself on the other axis.

Going back to the semiconductor industry, here are the situations occupied by the three major brands, based on how established they are, which can also be a substitute for market share, and whether they approach marketing from a factual (or "head") basis or a more emotional (or "heart") basis. From this, you can see how Intel saw the category for what it was, a typical engineering right-brain situation. The company went against the grain to carve out the dominant share in the computer-chip product category.

Owning conceptual space is a function of developing a compelling consumer benefit and an equally compelling personality. As categories become narrower and more similar from a consumer-benefit standpoint, the big difference may be in cultivating a unique brand personality. This maxim can apply to retailers, service companies, and business-to-business marketers, as well as to packaged-goods brands.

Defining What Business You Are In

Another way to approach a company that is not a traditional packaged-goods marketer is to ask the question, "What business are you in?" This seemingly innocuous question can really make for some interesting dialogue. Ted Leavitt's classic article "Marketing Myopia," pointed out two great examples from the mid-1900s. The first was the railroad industry, which viewed itself only within that context and not as a transportation alternative. The second was the motion picture industry, which viewed itself in the narrow realm of making movies; however, when television took hold, it had to change to a broader definition of entertainment.

The way to approach this exercise is similar to the way you ladder up the attributes from functional benefit to emotional benefit (see Chapter 5). The attribute in this case is the narrow view of the business. For example, the railroad industry is the product attribute. The benefit of the railroad is that it is a form of transportation. Perhaps the emotional benefit is that it is a form of transportation you can count on. So, you might be selling self-assurance.

Let's take a look at this perspective for a very low-interest category, the waste-services industry. The leader in the industry is Waste Management. The firm has a number of innovations whereby it turns waste into energy, it develops landfills so they can later be converted into golf courses, and it is the world's largest recycler of commodities. Of course, its trucks do pick up your trash. In looking at this company, you see it in the environmental-services business. While this may be the functional definition of the company, it has a much higher emotional definition. Waste Management "takes care of your world." By picking up the trash, it helps take care of your daily life, and by pushing innovative ways of disposing of trash, it is taking care of the world as a whole.

This exercise works well in the retail sector as well as in the B2B examples we have just given. For example, a furniture retailer may be in the home-furnishings business as a functional description of the furniture trade. However, it also may well be in the "self-expression" business from a consumer perspective. Consumers view furniture purchases like clothing items, a true expression of self. Getting a merchant-driven business to take this type of viewpoint usually is an eye-opener. It can have ramifications far beyond the way you might communicate to a customer.

Concept Testing

While you may slave away at defining the brand position of your product, it isn't worth any more than the paper it's written on if the consumer doesn't think it's compelling. Nor is it worth anything if it doesn't make for compelling advertising. So, how do we determine whether the positioning we have is truly compelling?

One method commonly used to help guide positioning, which at the same time can be used as input for advertising, is concept testing. Concept testing can consist of one or two elements. The first element is a copy block that sums up the brand's position in consumer-friendly copy. Rather than just saying "Dove is the brand of soap that leaves your face feeling refreshed because it has twice the moisturizing agents of any other soap," you might have a copy block that is more of a selling proposition, where you can test various ways of expressing the positioning statement to see what resonates with the consumer. For example, here are three ways of using this Ivory positioning statement to see what hits a chord with the consumers, moving from rational to more emotional.

1. You can trust your face to Dove because it has twice the moisturizing agents of any other soap.
2. You can always look your best with Dove because of its special moisturizing agents.
3. You take care of your body; Dove takes care of your face with its special moisturizing agents.

The advertising account planner might approach the positioning statement from many different directions to see how consumers feel about it. Many firms also couple the copy approach with a centering visual to create a two-page test. The right side of the page is the body copy while the left side of the page is a visual. The visual is important because consumers

Figure 7.3 **Hunt's Ketchup**

Hunt's Ketchup – Family Fun in Every Bottle!

When the whole family gathers for fun, casual meals there's often a bottle of Hunt's ketchup on the table!

Whether it's with your family, or friends in your backyard, Hunt's helps make meals more fun for everyone.

Families and friends have enjoyed the great Hunt's ketchup taste that comes from a recipe perfected over five generations.

Hunt's Ketchup for Fun Family Meals!

think more visually than auditorily. A visual gives you the opportunity to get at the consumers' "gut" reaction to something. Figure 7.3 is an example of such a concept board.

While it is up to the brand management team to finalize a brand's position, the account planner should make sure that position has some consumer relevancy. This is one way to test that position in the marketplace.

In summary, brand positioning is probably the single most important aspect of managing a brand. Much effort should be put on this exercise. Consumer packaged-goods marketers have pioneered this concept and are quite adept at honing a position. Business-to-business and retail marketers have different needs in this area. As an account planner, you need to adjust your thinking depending upon the product, good, or service with which you are involved.

Determining conceptual space or defining what business you are in is an offshoot of brand positioning that works well for B2B and retail companies. Proper brand positioning lays the groundwork for what we will discuss in the next chapter—how to communicate with the consumer.

Review Questions

1. How does positioning work? What alternative approaches might be used instead of positioning?
2. Can positioning be used for services as well as for products?
3. Can positioning be used for ideas? How? Give examples.
4. Does positioning relate more directly to benefits or to attributes in the promotional campaign?

Discussion Questions

1. What is the difference between a positioning strategy and an assault strategy?
2. What is the difference between positioning and the use of slogans or "tag lines"?
3. How do people position themselves?
4. How do politicians position themselves?
5. How can brand positioning be transferred into a personality matrix?

Exercises

1. Identify several brands and analyze their positions. For this exercise, you may want to select brands from the following categories: laundry detergents, toothpastes, airlines, automobiles, hair salons, and appliances.
2. Try to discern the personality matrix that might apply to each of these brands.
3. Are all the brands within a product category in the same "business," or can a brand create its own business segments and, thus, its own markets?

CBC Case Study

Go back to Chapter 1 to review the CBC case.

1. Using the CBC information from previous chapters, develop a positioning statement for CBC's products.
2. Next, use a brand personality matrix to analyze the CBC brand.
3. Now, define the business in which CBC operates. (Note: If this question seems overly simple, go back through this chapter and

review how a brand might be able to change the business sector in which it operates, or how it might even be able to create a new market segment.)

Additional Sources

Berry, John. *Tangible Strategies for Intangible Assets: How to Manage and Measure Your Company's Brand, Patents, Intellectual Property, and Other Sources of Value.* New York: McGraw-Hill, 2005.

Dearlove, Des. *Big Shots, Business the Richard Branson Way: 10 Secrets of the World's Greatest Brand Builder.* New York: Wiley, 2002.

Durkin, Dianne Michonski. *The Loyalty Advantage: Essential Steps to Energize Your Company, Your Customers, Your Brand.* New York: AMACOM, 2005.

Holt, Douglas B. *How Brands Become Icons: The Principles of Cultural Branding.* Boston, MA: Harvard Business School Press, 2004.

Leavitt, Ted. "Marketing Myopia." *Harvard Business Review* (July–August 1960): 45–56.

Chapter 8

The Creative Brief

It doesn't really matter whether you position a product correctly if you don't tell the consumers your story. Typically, this involves some sort of communication including, but not limited to, paid advertising.

As an account planner, it is your job to develop the creative brief, which serves as a platform for all the communications that the advertising agency or marketing communications firm may employ on behalf of the brand. Most account planners take great pride in their creative briefs. This item is the one tangible product they produce and is the most visible one to the advertising agency and its clients—as well as to one's colleagues.

In today's highly media-fragmented world, the creative brief takes on even greater importance than it did twenty or thirty years ago when there were a limited number of media outlets. The creative strategy is the "what to say" and the creative execution is the "how to say it." Both are extremely important to the success of an advertising campaign, yet follow very different ways of thinking. However, the media portion of the campaign has taken on an increasing importance within account planning, so the "where to say it" now has equal billing with the other two key areas of advertising communications strategy.

Much of creative strategy development uses what psychologists refer to as "convergent thinking." Convergent thinking is the process of drawing deductive and logical conclusions from the information at hand; thus, it goes from general to specific. This is an informational part of the process. Convergent thinking is used to distill the essence of the problem and to decide which particular piece of information or imagery will change consumers' behavior. Thus, it is a crucial part of developing the creative brief.

On the other hand, once a brief is fully developed, we enter into another phase of thinking called "divergent thinking." This style of thinking goes from specific to general: from the particular instances and situation to generalizations. This style of thinking is used by advertising creative departments to devise advertisements that will present this information or imagery in a fresh, new way.

While it is popular to paint advertising creative directors as rebels who are only interested in producing award-winning work, the majority of creative directors not only embrace creative strategy that is derived from a briefing document, but they demand it.

There is nothing more frustrating to a creative director than a loose or not-well-thought-out strategy. "Give me the freedom of a tight strategy" is a mantra heard at more than one advertising agency. The tighter or more detailed the strategy, the more the creative persons can stretch their minds to find an unusual way to communicate it. Again, because the stakes are high and the media landscape is so fragmented, the creative strategy must be crystal clear. Not only must it be absolutely clear, it must also inspire the creative product: the advertisements.

The issue of fragmentation also means that sometimes the creative brief is expanded into areas beyond the traditional creative department. In a normal situation, the advertising agency's creative brief is a document delivered to the creative teams, made up of an art director and a copywriter who are assigned to an account. This process worked well when everyone knew that television was the lead medium with print or radio as support vehicles. However, in today's world, there are a multitude of choices for paid media advertising and an equally daunting array of choices in nontraditional communications. Some examples of this are public relations events, sponsorships, cause marketing, interbrand cooperative marketing, and product integration. Interactive marketing has its own dizzying array of tactics including, but not limited to, search-engine marketing, online advertising, "blogs," and "podcasts."

While the media and communications landscape has changed, the basic components of delivering communications strategy have remained steady. They all boil down to the three legs of the stool: "What to say," "How to say it," and "Where to say it." Naturally, the floor for the stool, the foundation, is the consumer or the "who" in the equation.

Why Advertise at All?

This is a question that makes advertising agency management quiver. Yet as simple as it is, many times the advertiser and the advertising agency aren't on the same page about this question. More than half of the problems that develop between the two parties can be traced back to an issue of creative strategy. Put another way, there is often a lack of understanding about just what the advertising is intended to accomplish. For example, if a retailer is looking for immediate increases in store traffic but the advertising is a pure brand message designed for a longer term perception change, you will have a pending conflict over the results of the campaign. If everyone involved does not have a clear picture of what the goal is, it's little wonder there will be problems in evaluating the advertising agency's efforts to implement that strategy.

So before you get into a creative briefing session, you should sit together and draft a definition of the problem. This is where the account planner needs to take charge and lead the client. The client will likely say, "My problem is that sales are down" or "Customer traffic is soft." While it is true that this is a business problem, the reason sales are off is a consumer problem. So you need to frame the problem in consumer terms.

Let's take a look at an example for Pam Cooking Spray. The brand manager of Pam may see the sales for the brand eroding as private-label competitors' sales increase. The brand manager charges the advertising agency with fixing this problem. In consulting with the brand manager, the agency defines the problem, which is not as simple as "just getting consumers to buy more Pam Cooking Spray." The agency's definition of the problem that the advertising must solve is that consumers believe that Pam Cooking Spray isn't worth its premium price compared to private-label brands. Now you have an advertising problem to solve. In this case, it is convincing consumers that Pam Cooking Spray is worth the money. While the business problem is that fewer people are purchasing Pam Cooking Spray, the advertising problem is focused on the premium price differential between Pam and private-label cooking sprays. In this scenario, there may be a point where the price gap is too great between Pam and the alternatives, and all the advertising in the world may not be able to turn the tide on the brand's price-to-value equation.

That brings us back to the question of, "Why advertise at all?" Or perhaps a better question is, "Can advertising solve my problem?" For example, if you are charged with turning around a poor service perception of a retailer because the retailer has reduced the number and quality of its sales help, advertising isn't going to help. If anything, advertising may hurt the cause by bringing in more customers who will be disappointed in the reduced level of service.

Before you get to the creative briefing process, you should clearly define the business problem and the advertising problem to see whether advertising is the ingredient that can turn around the business problem. If advertising can't do it, you need the courage to say so. There is nothing worse than knowing you are going to fail right out of the gate. This does both you and your client a disservice.

Table 8.1

Early Creative Brief (Example: Pace Picante Sauce)

Key Fact
   Research shows that 70% of consumers think of Pace Picante Sauce as a dip
   for chips and not as a cooking ingredient

Problem that advertising must solve
   Convince consumers that Pace can be used for more than just chips

Advertising objective
   Educate consumers that Pace can be used in a variety of ways

The creative strategy
   Demonstrate that Pace can add zest to everyday recipes such as meatloaf,
   soups, and casseroles

Who, What, and Why of Communications

In its simplest form, a creative brief needs to deliver three things. To whom are you talking? Of what are you going to convince them? Why should they believe it? Much of this work comes directly from the positioning statement we worked on in the previous chapter.

In fact, some of the early creative briefs used in the 1960s and 1970s did not contain many more questions than were just listed. These early creative briefs were very linear in terms of the thinking involved. Most were influenced by the advertising agency Young & Rubicam, Inc. (Y&R). The Y&R style of creative brief usually had just four elements to it and worked in a sequential fashion. Table 8.1 is an example of an early creative brief that follows this sequence pattern.

Here, this creative brief began with a key fact. The key fact was a distillation of the research available on the brand and the market. The goal was to get the single nugget out of the research that was to be communicated. In the example of Pace Picante Sauce, the key fact was that 70 percent of consumers thought of Pace only as a dip for chips. Obviously, Pace wanted to broaden its product's usage appeal.

The second part of the brief was the problem that the advertising must solve. This is directly linked to the key fact. In the case of Pace, the problem was to convince consumers that Pace can be used in many more cooking occasions rather than just as a dip. This analysis led directly to the advertising objective, which was to educate consumers that Pace could be

Table 8.2

Typical Project Creative Brief

Question	Answer
What are we advertising?	Description of the product including all pertinent facts
Whom are we talking to?	Description of target audience
What is the objective?	Description of what the advertising is attempting to achieve
Where is the advertising running?	Schedule of media including types and sizes
What is the creative strategy?	A description of the selling proposition with rationale and copy points on product features and benefits
What else do we need to include in the advertising?	List of mandatories to be included, and list of items not to be included
When is the deadline?	Dates to review concepts and executions

used in a variety of ways. The creative strategy, then, was to demonstrate the other ways in which the product could be used.

Although this is a very iterative process, most advertising agencies that were dominated by large packaged-goods clients, such as Y&R, used this type of creative briefing process. It still has the fundamental building blocks of good communications strategies. What is conspicuously absent from these early creative briefs is any mention of target audience. In those days, there was a very large, mass audience; it was just assumed that the entire audience would be targeted. The other missing component was any mention of media; in those early days, television dominated the advertising media landscape and was a given for any mass-produced goods or wide-ranging services.

This early version of a creative brief gave way to a more complete creative brief that could be used for entire advertising campaigns as well as for individual advertisements or projects. Look at an example of the format for a typical creative brief that many advertising agencies use today (see Table 8.2).

This creative brief contains a less linear but more pragmatic view of the advertising process. It first begins with a description of the product being advertised, including the pertinent facts about the brand. This twist is another change of the key fact from the prior creative brief. Second, it moves on to discuss the target audience. The third point is the advertising objective, discussing what the advertising is designed to achieve. The fourth point is when the discussion of what media types and sizes should be used in the campaign is added to the equation. The fifth point is the creative strategy; this is a description of the selling proposition, including details on rationale and copy points. The sixth and seventh points are the most pragmatic and are usually found on creative project briefs. They include a list of mandatories, or "must-haves," such as legal copy or any other items that are essential in the advertising; finally, there is a discussion of due dates for the initial concept work and for the final executions (completed advertisement proposals).

You can see the difference between the early creative briefs and how they have been changed to include a better description of target market and to include media choices that would influence creative development. Both creative briefs would give creative art directors and writers a strong platform from which to ideate, but the latter approach incorporates tighter thinking and thus is more specific and more helpful.

Contemporary Creative Briefing

It is important to have a historical perspective on creative briefs and the briefing process. As we review a more recent creative brief, you can begin to see how the advertising process has grown more complex and more accountable. While the basics of a brief remain the same, there are some extremely big changes that have occurred over time.

The first change is not in the brief itself but in the way the brief is actually presented to the creative group. In earlier days of advertising, a creative brief was a dressed up "work order," requesting the creative group to "knock out" an advertising campaign. While it was done in a thoughtful manner, it was written up and delivered as part of the process. There were no fanfares or drum rolls accompanying it.

In today's advertising world, an advertising account planner is required not only to write a strategically sound brief but also to use the brief to inspire the creative group. There is as much thought that goes into selling the creative brief as there is in actually writing the creative brief. The "briefing" itself can have as much theater as the actual advertising that it generates.

While this may sound like we are pandering to "spoiled-brat" creatives, the advertising account planner should use this "briefing platform" to tell the story of the product within the context of the consumer target market. The passion that the account planner has for the strategy will be felt and reflected in the advertising outcomes. It is not unlike a coach selling his game plan to his team; if he isn't very excited about it, his team is not likely to get behind it. The same is true here. The account planner must give insight but also inspiration.

During this briefing process, it is crucial for the account planner to achieve three things with the creative group. The first goal is to paint a clear picture of whom the advertising will be targeting and what behavior is being expected as a result of the advertising. The second is to inspire the creative team to seek a novel solution to the problem and give the team a running start toward the solution. The third goal is to use the briefing as a quality control for ideas. You will not be the arbiter of the final creative product, but the creative work will have to pass through a strategic filter to be effective.

Contemporary Creative Brief

The creative briefing has changed over time and the creative brief itself has changed as well. One of the big changes is that the creative brief needs to direct a traditional creative team, an online team, a media team, and, perhaps, a marketing-services team. As a result, it needs to discuss some broad ways of how to reach the target market.

Another thing that has changed in the United States is the state of most consumer categories. The United States is a very mature market for many consumer goods. As a result, there are many brands and categories for which consumers have entrenched belief patterns. It is important to identify whether the beliefs about the brand are an impediment for getting to the behavior you desire, or whether something else must be communicated to convince consumers to do what you want. For example, Hunt's is the leading brand of tomato sauce. Consumers had a strong belief that it was the best on the market. Both quantitative and qualitative research indicated that Hunt's had the highest quality, yet sales were sagging. The solution was to get consumers to use the ingredient in new ways, not to convince them it was the best. They already believed in Hunt's quality, but the problem was to make Hunt's relevant to their day-to-day cooking needs. Understanding belief patterns is sometimes not enough in mature categories with mature brands that may need a different message to stimulate behavior.

The final aspect of the contemporary creative brief is that it includes a discussion of accountability. Now this concern may seem redundant, given that you are the person who set up the problem in the first place, yet it is important not only to understand what success is but also how it is measured. To the advertising agency, this component is vital: What is success? The agency managers and workers will want to understand how they are

Table 8.3

Contemporary Creative Brief

1. What is the problem?
2. Whom are we marketing to?
3. What do they currently believe?
4. What do we want them to do?
5. What can we do to motivate them?
   (a) What is the most compelling thing to say?
   (b) Where is the most compelling manner of conveying it?
6. What assets can we put toward this communication?
7. How will we measure success?
8. What are the mandatories?
9. What are the key milestones?

being measured. This becomes even more critical when part of the agency's compensation is on the line.

Let's take a look at the brief and walk through each aspect of it (see Table 8.3).

What Is the Problem?

The first part of the creative brief is similar to the early creative brief and that is "the problem we must solve." You will note in this contemporary brief that the problem is not stated as "the problem advertising must solve." In this case, the solution could be much more than advertising, so we do not want the problem to be constrained only to advertising solutions. In today's marketing communications world, there are myriad tactical options to solve a problem. What we want to see is the problem stated in some sort of consumer language. "Sales are soft" is a problem, but what we need to know in this case is the "why." Consumers may not be buying as much Dove soap as in the past because they believe all soaps are basically the same. Now this is a problem to solve.

Whom Are We Marketing to?

This is a reprise of our discussion back in Chapter 5. When you describe to whom you are marketing, it should be more than just a demographic description. It should include consumer motivations. Your goal here is to paint a succinct picture of the consumer so that whoever is trying to help you solve the problem should understand those potential customers very well.

It is not adequate to suggest that the target market is women who buy disposable diapers or engineers who specify silicon chips. You need to offer up not only who they are, but also what they need. This is when you draw upon the need state to paint the picture. For example, a finicky mom who always wants the best for her child tells you something about the disposable-diaper buyer. Senior engineers who crave to be at the leading edge of their profession tell you something about these persons who need computer chips. Draw out to whom it is you are marketing.

What Do They Currently Believe?

This is what Tom Monroe, chief creative officer (CCO) at FogartyKlein-Monroe, calls defining the brand's "mirror image." It should be a reflection of what consumers believe about the brand as it stands. The image may be a great one like the case of Hunt's tomato sauce or it may be a poor one. Convincing consumers to shop at Kmart, after the retail chain has declared bankruptcy a second time, may be a different story. As the advertising account planner, your role here is to editorialize about the brand as seen through the eyes of the consumers. It is more than simply to report the data.

Within this statement you should cover some diagnostic ground. You need to cover the awareness of the brand, preferences of consumers, and any barriers, which the current set of belief patterns to the brand have, that relate to buying the brand more often. You want to cover any and all beliefs held about the brand and relate them to the problem you are facing.

What Do We Want Them to Do?

This is the $64,000 question. What is the outcome you want from the consumers? Typically, this outcome is a behavioral issue. You might want them to change behavior; for example, you might want them to switch from buying Dove soap to buying Dial soap. Or you might want them to use your soap product more often. Or you might want to get someone who doesn't use soap to try it. All of these situations are pretty standard behaviors, and while these examples are packaged-goods oriented, they can work for retailers as well.

In applying this step to a B2B situation, you might be asking for a different outcome. It might be to include your company within the considered set for a RFP (request for proposal), which is a solicitation for a contract. It might be to see a sales representative or to call a 1-800 number. As at the consumer-marketing level, you are looking for the best outcome.

We have focused on behavior, but this outcome can also be about what customers think. If you identify the problem and belief pattern as an issue, then the outcome might be to think differently than in the past. For example, you might want someone to consider that a Mercedes-Benz is a good value rather than an expensive luxury car.

The importance of this question cannot be overestimated, because this is "where the rubber meets the road," where the facts and figures and goals must be specific and applicable. Whatever you want someone to do as a result of the communications should be measurable. If it is measurable, then it will have some monetary value. You should craft this statement as if you were writing your compensation agreement because, in essence, that is exactly what you are doing.

What Can We Do to Motivate Action?

What Is the Most Compelling Thing to Say?

We need to find what to say, something that will motivate someone to take the course of action that we have identified. This is the basis of communications strategy. It could be the key benefit, a way of meeting the consumers' need state. It could be some new information about the product that is a compelling reason why they should buy the product. Whatever the nugget is, here is where you deliver it. This point is where you outline the reason why this is the most compelling thing to say.

Where Is the Most Compelling Place to Convey It?

Here, you should introduce a discussion about communications venues. Because this brief goes to media, public relations, online specialists, and other professional communicators, this is a place to give some thought to all forms of communication. They can be traditional media vehicles, such as television or newspapers, or nontraditional media, such as video games, cell phones, or the Internet. They can also be nonpaid media, such as special events or "viral" marketing campaigns that can start on a small basis and then spread like a rumor on the school or business "grapevine." The goal of this section is to stretch the boundaries on thinking about how to contact the consumer.

What Are the Assets We Can Put Toward This Communication?

In this section, you will cover the budget items. If there are separate budgetary line items for media and production, they can be covered here. This is also a good place to add any communications items or avenues that the brand might already have in place for communications; these could be existing or potential channels, such as signs, trucks, affiliations, sponsorships, newsletters, billing statements, tray liners, or any other form of communications that the advertiser might have with the consumer.

How Will We Measure Success?

This is the discussion of how we are going to measure the action we are trying to create, how we will judge the impact and effect. If we are measuring retail traffic, then we should put that goal in this section. If there is primary research, perhaps tracking the motivations of consumers, then it can go here as well. It might be wise, as the account planner, for you to hold a "success" meeting with the brand managers. Understanding the measurement success will help you unlock the potential of what you are trying to do.

What Are the Mandatories and What Are the Key Milestones?

These two questions are the necessary wrap-up items that include the mandatories we discussed previously in this chapter, as well as the due dates for each step of the process.

As you can see, the contemporary creative brief is really a broader communications-briefing process. It includes a distinctive marketing bent with a broad definition of the problem as well as a discussion of results. However, it is more expansive in the area of strategies, with both creative and media strategies discussed in the same brief. In the next chapter, however, we shall discuss the possible need to have a more fully developed media brief.

In summary, creative briefs have changed over time in response to a more complicated media landscape and a more complex consumer marketplace. However, these are the exact reasons why a communications brief, advertising brief, and creative brief are even more important today than ever before.

The remedy for complexity lies in being simple and focused. The communications-briefing document is a way of gaining focus and having the entire advertising agency marching to the beat of the same drummer—working together collaboratively toward the same goals.

Review Questions

1. How does a creative brief differ from a copy platform?

2. Why does a creative brief need to match up with the positioning? Why have both a positioning statement and a creative brief?
3. What does a creative brief have to do with an advertising message approach?
4. What does the message approach have to do with the advertising media approach?

Discussion Questions

1. If a marketer has done a good job of market research, would a creative brief also be needed? Why?
2. In preparing advertising messages, why not just begin writing or designing or illustrating the advertisement?
3. Is the creative brief expressed in words only? Can it involve both words and pictures? Can it also involve layout and design?
4. How do convergent thinking and divergent thinking relate to the logical research processes of inductive and deductive reasoning?

Exercises

1. Select several advertisements from print media (newspapers and magazines). Look at the advertisements and try to work backwards to figure out the creative briefs for each advertisement. Why do you think these approaches were used? (Although this exercise can be applied to any advertising medium, using print media allows several people to analyze the advertisements at the same time, and print advertisements are easier to collect than are broadcast or interactive media messages.)
2. Using the same collection of print-media advertisements, try to guess what kinds of research might have been conducted to result in these advertising-message approaches.
3. Still using the same collection of advertisements, analyze why these particular advertising media were selected for carrying their specific advertising messages.

CBC Case Study

Refer to the CBC case from Chapter 1.

1. Using what you have analyzed and proposed from the previous steps in this case, now develop a creative brief for the CBC brand.

2. Make sure that your creative brief differentiates CBC from its competitors and that it properly includes the intended audience as well as the proper media selections.

Additional Sources

De Bonis, Nicholas J., and Roger S. Peterson. *AMA Handbook for Managing Business to Business Marketing Communications*. New York: McGraw-Hill, 1997.

Du Plessis, Erik. *The Advertised Mind: Ground-Breaking Insights into How Our Brains Respond to Advertising*. London: Kogan Page Business Books, 2005.

Lewis, Herschell Gordon. *Advertising Age: Handbook of Advertising*. New York: McGraw-Hill, 1998.

Prather, Charles, and Lisa Gundry. *Blueprints for Innovation: How Creative Processes Can Make You and Your Company More Competitive*. New York: AMACOM, 1995.

Steel, Jon. *Truth, Lies, and Advertising: The Art of Account Planning*. New York: Wiley, 1998.

Vicker, Lauren, and Ron Hein. *The Fast Forward MBA in Business Communication*. New York: Wiley, 1999.

Chapter 9

Media and Account Planning

Inherently, advertising account planning has been a task that combines much more directly with advertising creative development than with advertising media-plan development. Recently, however, there has been a movement in the advertising industry to have account planners or media professionals with an account-planning bent work on advertising media strategy as well as on creative strategy.

This movement toward having advertising account planners work with media groups on media strategy is the result of some fundamental changes in the media landscape. One rather obvious change is that advertising media options have dramatically escalated over the past ten years. We are now in an age where the average U.S. consumer has access to eighty cable television channels, twenty or more radio stations, thousands of magazines and newspapers, and infinite online opportunities. The "old" outdoor advertising industry is transforming itself into an out-of-home medium, with digital billboards that look more like television than outdoor, plus a dizzying array of place-based vehicles ranging from trademarks in the sand at a beach to logos drawn on people's foreheads. These days, it seems that anything that can be an advertising medium.

Another fundamental shift in media is happening as this book is being written. This change now puts the consumers in control of their media choices. The days of advertisers pushing content to the consumers is rapidly coming to a close. The consumers are now in a position to choose what they want to watch or read and when they want to watch or read it. Technological advances, like TiVO and DVR (digital video recorder), are making big inroads in the consumer media arena. Satellite radio is stirring up the once-staid radio arena, so consumers can now select from countless channels and musical formats in their cars or homes. The computer is now the centerpiece of a digital revolution, impacting the way advertising will be transmitted and received in the future.

The Account Planning Role in Media

With all the changes in media, the role of the advertising account planner in advertising media strategy is to help the media teams understand what medium is most engaging to the consumer for the brands they are marketing. Media are moving from mass reach and high efficiency to niche-audience layers that offer effective audience-member engagement.

Even with this seismic shift, advertising media still represent the bastion of cost efficiencies, reach, and frequency, and a number of quantitative measures that aid an advertiser in achieving an effective plan. As an account planner, your role is not to determine whether the media are efficient or whether you can negotiate a better deal; your role is to look at the world of media from a consumer's viewpoint. You are there to help the media group dimensionalize the target market and to add insight into where the consumer might be the most susceptible to receiving the advertising messages.

Let's take a look at some of the larger areas where account planning has made a difference in media planning.

Melding Target Markets

Much of advertising success is involved in linking the creative work with the media plan. It does no good if the creative group is designing a campaign to convince cooks who don't currently use cooking spray to try your brand while the media group is reaching out to existing heavy users of cooking spray. Although this seems like a "no-brainer," it happens every day because media and creative groups are many times in different companies, and even when they are within the same walls, historically, they have very little contact.

This is an important area where the account planner can help. You can be the bridge between these two groups. A great place to start is in the area of the target market. Your role is to help meld the qualitative needs of the creative group with the quantitative needs of the media group.

The media group typically uses demographics as the primary source of the target definition. In the case of cooking spray users, a media target might be defined as:

Women, age 35–54, with HHI $50,000+

From there, the media group would go off and look for media and vehicles that efficiently reach this group.

What if you added this description to the demographic target: "Women who love to cook and seek out cooking tips and hints from the media"? Now what is more important to you as a marketer, the demographic de-

Table 9.1

Target Considerations: Manwich Sloppy Joe Mix

Target Considerations		Media Implications
Women 25–54, with kids, national	➡	National TV plan
Purchase is in grocery channel with Wal-Mart dominant distributor	➡	Review Wal-Mart TV network or parking lot boards
Moms view Manwich as fun meal with family	➡	Look at "Funtime" TV shows with entire family viewing
Finding Manwich in store can be daunting task	➡	Look at testing in-store graphics
Average purchase is every 2 to 3 weeks with no large seasonal skews	➡	Recency plan makes sense

scription or this behavioral description? The correct answer is the latter. Why? Because it is a true marketing target while the former is a demographic description of a target market. This is not a semantic game. If the medium of choice for this campaign is magazines, the demographic target may yield publications such as *Reader's Digest, Family Circle,* or *Good Housekeeping.* These are large-circulation print-media vehicles that have a low cost per thousand for this target demographic. While these publications may reach the target and may contain articles of interest in varying degrees, a publication such as *Cooking Light* might be more of a bull's eye. Here is a magazine chocked full of cooking tidbits that would appeal to your target market and would fit the creative approach that you are devising.

The point is that the account planner must add some behavioral dimensions to the target market description so that both the media and creative groups are synchronizing their efforts. Sometimes this can be as easy as ensuring the target is defined as heavy, medium, or light users, or nonusers, of a particular product category. This alone helps get everyone on board, but it does not get after the motivation for why the consumers act the way they do. If the motivation for the consumers in the cooking spray example is to provide a healthier meal for their families, then placing advertisements in a nurturing environment may be a trigger to have women respond to the advertising.

As an account planner, you need to provide the details necessary for the media group to develop media analysis. This includes demographics and usage information, but you also need to provide other aspects to the target as well, such as consumer motivation, helping the media group hit the bull's eye with the plan (see Table 9.1).

How Media Fit into an Audience's Life

Another aspect of media planning is finding out the best time to get a message to a consumer. The time when the consumer is most susceptible to the message is called "susceptibility." If you could buy advertising on the mirror into which a woman looks in the morning to put on her make-up, that would be an opportune moment for any cosmetic company to advertise.

You can't always find these moments, but as an account planner it is your role to offer consumer insights to the media group on when the consumer would be most receptive to your advertiser's message. It might involve intercepting the consumers at a specific time of day or at a specific place, or when they are likely to be with someone special. All of these insights into the consumers' lifestyle and how they consume media are critical to media strategy.

A great example of media and creative groups working together to define a solution can be found with Brink's Home Security. The consumer insight was that most people felt safe when they were at home and had more fears about their home being burglarized when they were away from it. The creative group developed a campaign talking about "being there when you aren't." The media group used radio as the primary medium and placed advertisements when consumers were most likely to be driving around, away from home. The results of the campaign were staggering. Together, the media and creative groups had hit a nerve in terms of communicating when consumers were most susceptible to the advertising.

How the Brand Is Bought

How the brand is purchased is a key question to look at in terms of the target audience, and it also may have media implications. It can also be a difficult question to answer definitively. For example, if the brand is a can of beans, we know it is purchased, typically, at a grocery store. However, is it usually an impulse purchase or is it a part of an every-two-weeks ritual? Depending on the answer, the media planner can develop totally different plans.

If it is a service, does a salesman sell it to you or can you buy it on the Internet? Is it something you buy because your parents have recommended it? Or is it something you have spent the past six months researching? Knowing the "ins and outs" of the purchase process is a crucial piece of information that can materially impact the advertising media plan. This type of data is vital to a media planner who is considering not only how the brand may fit into the consumer's life but how the consumer goes about purchasing it in the first place.

This type of information also goes well beyond just knowing the product's purchase cycle. Here, the account planner is looking for consumer insight that will offer the media planners a story for developing their contact plan.

The rise of floor graphics in the grocery store is a direct response to the impulsive nature of many food purchases. Floor graphics have a big effect on sales of snacks and beverages, which are much more impulse items to purchase than are staples such as milk or butter.

Knowing that purchasing auto insurance has significantly shifted from seeking an agent in the Yellow Pages to searching the Internet for the best deal has markedly changed marketing spending in this huge category. Now, advertisers put a considerable amount of effort into search-engine and keyword searches as a critical part of their media spending, rather than just relying on the Yellow Pages to present the message. This is the result of a consumer change in the market.

The Media Work Plan

Just like the creative group, the media group works off the same briefing document. You may elect to use the communications brief we discussed in the previous chapter as a media brief. However, many media companies and advertising agencies have their own media brief that is agreed to by the client in the same manner as the creative brief.

In the case of media, there is some very specific information that media professionals need in order to develop a smart media plan. Let's review the basic information required to develop a traditional media plan.

1. The budget is a critical element in the plan. In this case, the media planner is looking only at the media budget portion of the total advertising or marketing budget. It is important to note whether the budget contains agency commission (gross) or does not (net). Many times there may be different commission structures by medium, which the client has negotiated with the media planning or buying partners, so always be careful when filling out this part of the work plan.

2. The planner also needs specific start and end dates to be able to schedule the media plan. It is important to note the client's fiscal year, as this sometimes dictates patterns of spending that the media planner should take into account.

3. Similar to the creative group, media planners need some detailed background that tells them the purpose of the campaign, whether there is new or existing creative work involved, and whether there are any predetermined media ideas or "musts" for the campaign. The background can also contain any competitive insights that may offer the planner an innovative way of standing out in the category.

4. The planner needs to know how the brand is bought. Is it purchased in a store, or online, or through the mail? Who buys the brand and is it the same person who is actually using the brand? This is the area of the work plan where the account planner can add the most value, so give a thorough description of this activity.

5. Media planning is a lot like putting a puzzle together. Media planners need to know key market facts, such as the brand's seasonality of purchase, its market strengths and weaknesses, where it is distributed, and where the competitors are spending their money. All of these elements lead the planner to recommend a type of allocation strategy.

6. The media planners need to know the target audience at which they are aiming. This target description needs to be both fact-based, with demographic data, as well as psychology-based, so the planner can make judgments on what media best link up with the target market. From these data, the media planner will recommend a buying target for the execution of the media plan.

7. The media planner needs to know whether there are any mandatories or "sacred cows" with the plan. Did the client already commit to a sponsorship? Or is it important to buy the news broadcast to reach the trade, or is the client's girlfriend the publisher of a magazine?

8. Any creative considerations should be spelled out. Is this an existing or new advertising campaign? Are there specific creative units that have been developed, or is one of the roles of the media planner to aid in coming up with the optimum creative unit mix?

9. How success is measured is also a key component of the media plan. This should be spelled out as to how and when measurements will be made, because this can impact scheduling of media. See Table 9.2 for an example of a media work plan.

Balancing Efficiency and Effectiveness

Media planning is largely a trade-off between cost efficiency and effectiveness in reaching the predescribed target market. This is particularly true in

Table 9.2

Media Work Plan

Client:	Brand:	Date:
Media budget only (net/gross):	Campaign start:	Campaign end:
	Plan due internally:	Plan due to client:

1. Background (what is the situation facing the brand?)

2. Advertising objectives

3. Target audience (list marketing target, including any relevant attitudinal, demographic, and psychographic date)

4. How is the brand bought? (list factors on how it is purchased, such as target influencers or timing, that could aid in media planning)

5. Key marketing factors
   (a) Seasonality
   (b) Geography (BDI/CDI)
   (c) Distribution
   (d) Competition

6. Creative considerations (new or existing campaigns)

7. Mandatories

8. Measurement

media negotiations, where a media negotiator's job is to get the most for the money available. Unless given very tight buying parameters, a media negotiator will usually sacrifice the target richness of a media vehicle for a more cost-efficient one. This situation is particularly true in broadcast negotiations, where the choices are great and the pressure to deliver a certain cost per thousand (CPM) is high.

As an account planner, your role is not to negotiate a media buy; that's the media buyer's job. Your role is to meet with the members of the media negotiation team to make sure they understand the target market and will put a premium on delivering this particular audience. A savvy account planner can also help the media negotiation team by paving the way with the clients, helping them understand that it might not be in their best interests to err on the efficiency side of the equation.

For some brands, where the target market is a heavy consumer of media, cost efficiency rules the day. But for brands having a more discriminating media audience, you can "cut off your nose to spite your face" by not putting the priority on effectiveness in reaching the target market, over the priority of efficiency.

The Issue of Reach

A fundamental dimension to the media-planning discussion is the issue of reach. Reach can be looked at in a number of ways. There is vertical reach, which is the number of consumers you reach on a weekly, monthly, or annual basis. There is also horizontal reach, which is the number of weeks you are advertising or the percentage of time you are covering. Figure 9.1 shows a sample of a reach matrix.

Media planners have much more sophisticated analysis than this to bring to the issue of reach, but as an account planner, your goal is to make sure the media planner is moving in the right direction. A discussion about reach, using the matrix in Figure 9.1, is a good conceptual starting ground for the media team and the client to understand how best to weigh vertical versus horizontal reach.

For example, if you were introducing a new sandwich for McDonald's that is at a "sharp" price "point" for a month, you would want to weigh vertical reach much more heavily than horizontal reach. Your goal would be to tell as many people as possible about it in the shortest amount of time. You would want a much more impact-heavy schedule for your advertising support.

Conversely, if you were continuing to build awareness for Kraft Macaroni and Cheese, then you might weigh horizontal reach more heavily than vertical reach. In this case, you may want more of a recency strategy than an impact strategy.

In summary, media planning is a very detailed field requiring a strong marketing sense. However, as an account planner, you can help media professionals shape their plans by providing more contexts about the consumers they are trying to reach effectively and efficiently. The description of the target market, plus a thorough briefing on how the brand is purchased, is a big aid to media planners as they tackle a plan. An understanding of the trade-offs between pure cost efficiency and target-rich media vehicles can aid the understanding of both the media negotiators and the advertiser as they work to allocate their advertising dollars for maximum results.

Figure 9.1   **Reach Matrix**

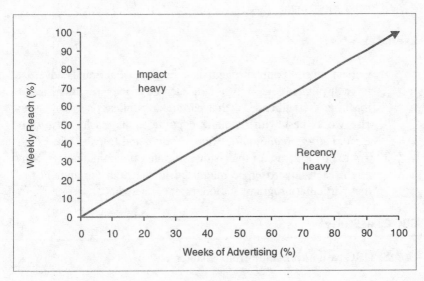

Review Questions

1. How many kinds of marketing targets are there? Why is more than one type of target necessary?
2. How does target selection affect account planning?
3. To what degree must positioning match up with media selection, and vice versa?
4. What are the differences between quantitative and qualitative factors in advertising media? What are examples of each?

Discussion Questions

1. What is lifestyle? What does lifestyle have to do with the purchase of products or services?
2. Which aspects of marketing can be controlled? Which cannot be controlled? Why?
3. What is meant by "extending the media"? Why is this concept important?
4. Which advertising media factors are quantitative? Which are qualitative?

5. What kinds of products and service need "vertical" reach? Which need "horizontal" reach?

Exercises

1. Collect several popular magazines. Look at what brands advertise in each publication. Why might each advertiser be interested in reaching the audience of that particular publication? (This exercise works best with specialized publications, such as *Cooking Light, Cargo, Real Simple, Men's Health,* and *Car & Driver.*)
2. Try to do the same for television programs and commercials. Why might each advertiser be interested in reaching the audience of that particular program, station, or cable network?

CBC Case Study

Use the CBC case information from Chapter 1.

1. Select the targets for your advertising campaign for CBC.
2. Select the media characteristics that you would seek to use for advertising CBC.
3. Now select actual types of media that you would use for the advertising campaign for CBC.
4. Finally, select actual media vehicles that you might use for the CBC advertising.

Additional Sources

Butterfield, Leslie. *Advalue: Twenty Ways Advertising Works for Business.* Oxford; Boston: Butterworth-Heinemann, 2003.
Farbey, David. *How to Produce Successful Advertising: A Guide to Strategy, Planning and Targeting.* London: Kogan Page, 1994.
Myers, Greg. *Adworlds: Brands, Media, Audiences.* London: Arnold, 1999.
Turow, Joseph. *Breaking Up America: Advertisers and the New Media World.* Chicago: University of Chicago Press, 1997.
Wells, William, D. *Measuring Advertising Effectiveness.* Hillsdale, NJ: Lawrence Erlbaum, 1997.

Chapter 10
Measuring Success

What is the measure of success for your marketing or advertising campaign? The answer to that question may depend largely on whom you ask. The creative director may say, "To win a Clio." The marketing director may say, "To increase sales." The CEO of the company may say, "To protect my margin, which helps drive shareholder value." And the account manager at the advertising agency may say, "To keep the account happy."

So, which one of these is right? Perhaps they are all right. Or perhaps just one is right. Therein lies the challenge with measuring success. It all depends upon your agenda and viewpoint. More often than not, not everyone will be on the same page. Aligning all the stakeholders to work together is an important facet of any marketing communications program.

In fact, as the advertising account planner, you have a unique vantage point from which to help both the company and the advertising agency agree on what success should be and how it should be measured. Both what success should be and how it should be measured are equally important. It does no good to agree on what is important and then not have the proper way of measuring it. Obviously, the converse is true as well; you can have a great research instrument that may not get at the most relevant issue. In this chapter, we will deal both with defining success and with the appropriate measures for researching the results.

Defining Success

There may be no meeting that you conduct more important than the "success meeting." Every account planner should request this meeting, preferably prior to the beginning of planning a SWOT analysis and certainly well before a creative brief is in the hands of the creative department. Understanding what the definition of success is will clearly pave the way for you to attack the problem at hand.

A "success meeting" may not necessarily be a roundtable discussion. However, you should gather the viewpoint of the CEO, the leadership committee of the company, and the marketing group. Depending upon your access to the company, it can also be helpful to interview representatives from the board of directors. Your role in this process is to understand where the company is coming from and then to go through their wish lists of success criteria.

Once you understand the company, you may want to draft a "success statement" that everyone agrees to and supports. In this statement, you list the criteria that the marketing or advertising campaign should have as a goal.

This is also a good time to help all the stakeholders understand the link between marketing investment and return on investment. The true strength of building a brand is largely the psychological strength of the brand in the minds of the consumers. This is not to say that short-term sales cannot be a goal. However, if your goals are only short-term sales, then you are missing the point of making an ongoing marketing investment, which is to strengthen the brand and make it less vulnerable to competition.

Take a look at the compilation of brand strengths: the brand potential index (see Figure 10.1). It is a nice place to start the dialogue with the company on what you are trying to achieve with your marketing expenditures.

The discussion of "success" should largely be a discussion of brand value and increasing the brand's valuation. As the brand-strength wheel describes, there are a number of key measures that you might discuss about what you are ultimately attempting to accomplish. The end result of your accomplishments should be to strengthen the brand. One of the most powerful aspects of building a successful brand is the ability to command a premium price for the brand and to command brand loyalty even in the wake of price increases. As a marketer, you want consumers to be willing to pay a premium price for your brand and to be fanatically loyal to the brand. Any CEO will tell you that the ability to gain a greater margin on the competitors' sales is the hallmark of a well-run company. These are the companies that command a higher price multiple on the stock market. Brand strength certainly equates to company strength.

In today's marketplace, Starbuck's commands this position where consumers are willing to pay over $3 for a 50-cent cup of coffee and will blindly go past a myriad of alternatives to satisfy their thirst for Starbuck's. Everyone should be this lucky. Starbuck's has worked its magic in this market. The chain has based its strategy on developing a meeting place serving coffee, rather than just focusing on the coffee itself. By changing the game, Starbuck's wins on all fronts.

Success can also be just simple things, like gaining brand penetration or purchase frequency among current users. It may be getting a current user to

Figure 10.1   **Brand Potential Index**

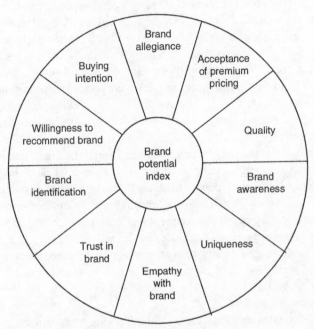

recommend the brand to another person. This is a key measure of real estate success, and for that matter, success in just about any service business. The challenge may be more of a perception problem. Perhaps your brand is not perceived as being unique or distinctive. It may have a poor quality perception or people may just simply not be aware of it. Whatever the measure of success, you should "nail it down" so all parties agree and get focused behind the solution.

Again, a discussion of success will cover the core aspects of the brand. Once you have everyone "buy in" on what success should be, then you can develop the proper tools to measure it. We will take a look at some of these tools in this chapter, recognizing that this will not be a comprehensive discussion of research.

Tracking Studies

Tracking results can involve a variety of methods. There are two basic tracking areas. The first is a sort of sales tracking, or a method to track purchasing behavior. The second revolves around understanding how consumers view the brand from an attitudinal perspective. The first represents the hard facts of money and the second represents the more elusive perceptions.

All companies track their sales to varying degrees of detail. A restaurant usually tracks the traffic count and average check amount, which is their vernacular for how many customers came to dine and what was the average amount they spent. Variations of this traffic count and average sale are the hallmarks of most retail tracking. In packaged-goods marketing, there are syndicated tools such as A.C. Nielsen and IRI, providing packaged-goods manufacturers with a rolling tally of unit sales. Because these systems are often linked to consumers through shopping cards, there is a wealth of data available to tell the manufacturer who is purchasing the brand and whether it was purchased using a coupon or an in-store special deal. Packaged-goods manufacturers use "penetration" and "buy rate" as their two primary behavioral measures. Penetration is how many different consumers purchase the brand; buy rate is the frequency of purchase. Even B2B sales are tracked by customer and average sale. Business-to-business sales are also evaluated based on gross margin, or how much each sale contributes to the company's profits. All companies attempt to measure market share, or how much they are getting of the entire consumer-spending "pie" for their product or service categories.

While these sales measures are ongoing tracking studies in and of themselves, they are not what marketers call tracking studies. Tracking studies are primary research studies measuring the consumer's awareness of, attitudes toward, and intent to use the brand or company in question. They are sometimes called AAU (Awareness, Attitude, and Usage) studies. These studies are measures of consumer perception but not necessarily of behavior. While sales tracking measures actual consumer behavior, an AAU study is measuring the consumer's attitudinal perception of the brand. Each is a crucial component to understanding how the consumer is interacting and will interact with the brand.

There are two basic ways to conduct a tracking study. One method is to do a pre- and postmeasure study. This type of study surveys consumers before the advertising begins and then again at some designated point after the advertising has been scheduled or run. Most marketers do this type of survey work either every quarter, every six months, or annually. These types of studies are quantitative in nature and have large sample sizes to determine whether there is statistically significant movement in areas of the brand that are perceptual in nature. For example, if you survey a thousand consumers before the advertising runs and find that 20 percent are aware of your brand, then conduct a survey of another random thousand consumers six months after the advertising runs and you find that 30 percent of consumers are aware of the brand, you would have a statistically significant movement at a 95-percent (or 0.05) confidence level.

However, this pre- and postmeasurement method for tracking results can be problematic, depending upon the timing of the study and what else is going on in the marketplace. This is particularly true for a brand or category frequently purchased, such as potato chips or bread, where there are considerable changes in the marketing landscape on a weekly basis. If you pick a point in time when your competitors are aggressively spending or have taken some significant marketing action, such as a price-incentive program, then you may get a distorted view of the postwave results. If you survey directly after the advertising flight, compared against a period after a month-long hiatus period, you are likely to get different results. Depending upon the results, the advertiser and the agency may quibble for weeks on end about the validity of the results and their implications for the future.

To mitigate this problem, Millward Brown, a UK research company with a large U.S. presence, came up with a continuous-tracking method that has been widely adopted in today's marketing circles. This method is used by many other marketing research firms to track advertising impact in the marketplace. It is a favored method of packaged-goods brands, while service companies and B2B marketers usually maintain a more traditional pre- and postmeasurement measurement method. A continuous tracker surveys the consumer base every week, usually with a minimum of a fifty-person weekly sample base but sometimes smaller. This information is then rolled up into a quarterly report of 600 or more respondents, which is similar to the sample size for quarterly tracking reports. The difference is that, in the continuous tracker, you can see weekly variance in the measures you are studying and correlate those with any changes in the marketplace.

When a continuous tracker is combined with a weekly sales tracking device, you have a powerful diagnostic tool to determine how marketing and advertising is impacting sales and brand values. Figure 10.2 is an example of a continuous tracking scenario, where brand purchase is correlated with a new advertising campaign.

While most companies are concerned with sales and the impact that marketing has on them, there are also other important success variables that warrant close consideration. For example, if your success goal is to be perceived as the best can of beans and worth the price, then studying the quality relationship between your brand and that of the competitors' may be the key item to pay attention to in tracking. Likewise, if you are a retailer and maintaining a high level of service is your bailiwick, then

Figure 10.2   **Brand A: Key Measurement Summary of Continuous Tracker**

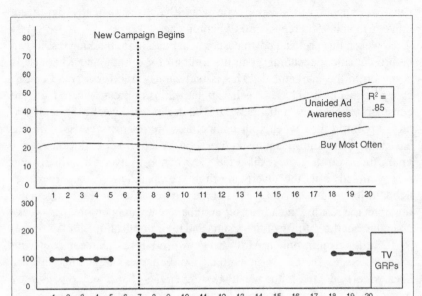

your service perception versus that of competitors may be the top item you evaluate. Business-to-business marketers are typically concerned about being in the consideration set and how their values match up with the competition.

Tracking studies are a good tool to monitor how the brand is performing on the agreed-to success measures. Most marketers conduct traditional tracking studies for their companies once, twice, or four times a year. While these research "snapshots" can provide good information, if the company or brand can afford a continuous tracking study, it will typically yield a more comprehensive look at the brand's situation and what variables impact it.

Marketing Mix Modeling

Because of the technological developments in tracking sales data, there is a tremendous rise in the number of marketers attempting to correlate sales not only with advertising but also with specific tactics within the entire marketing mix. Driven largely by packaged-goods marketers, Marketing

Table 10.1

Marketing Mix Model: Bob's Beans

Item	Incremental profit (per $1.00 spent)
Media advertising	1.50
FSI coupons	1.00
Trade promotions	0.85

Source: Larry Kelley and Donald Jugenheimer, *Advertising Media Planning: A Brand Management Approach.* Armonk, NY: M.E. Sharpe, Inc., 2003, p. 91. Reprinted with permission.

Mix Modeling (MMM) uses econometric modeling techniques to understand what factors contribute the most to sales.

These marketing heuristics are more available today than ever before because of the endless supply of grocery-scanner data, allowing marketers to analyze very granular (i.e., tiny) pieces of information. Using two years of data and more than a hundred observations, an econometric model can be developed that helps to explain well over 70 percent of sales and upwards to 90 percent of sales via the three large components of marketing activity for a grocery brand: advertising, consumer promotions, and trade promotions. All of these models use sophisticated multivariate statistical analysis with senior research personnel manning these intricate models.

This type of analysis has taken hold, particularly in the advertising media departments that already have a quantitative bent. In our book *Advertising Media Planning: A Brand Management Approach,* there is a good example of a marketing mix exercise for a fictitious product, Bob's Baked Beans. In this example, we see that our fictitious brand, Bob's Baked Beans, is extremely sensitive to advertising (see Table 10.1). For every dollar that Bob's spends on media advertising, the brand receives a return of $1.50. As you can see from Table 10.1, this is a much higher return than from the other aspects of the marketing mix, such as FSI (free-standing insert) coupons or trade promotions. Based on this analysis, you would likely suggest that Bob's Baked Beans conduct a heavy-spending test to see where the threshold is for the brand's media weight.

The majority of packaged-goods marketers are doing MMM, and media departments of advertising agencies or media companies are involved in the development of these models as they relate to specific media variables, such as media mix, media weight levels, and "flighting" patterns.

As an advertising account planner, your role in MMM is not to get out your college statistics books to figure out the dynamics of sales and advertising. Leave the "number crunching" to the research professionals. Your mission is to understand that this kind of detailed research is possible and to encourage its use as a learning tool. Management likes quantitative tools, but you should also understand the limitations of MMM. Just because it can explain the past is no guarantee that it will be able to explain the future. In fact, many marketers are attempting to develop dynamic models that can explain sales correlations in "real time" so that they can make more astute decisions.

Also, while statistics don't lie, liars use statistics. While MMM and any sales-modeling exercises are very important, they don't always tell you the full story or complete truth. It is hard to "tease" or conjure out of a model what may be the emotional impact of a marketing idea. Models are focused on short-term sales results and not on building long-term brand strengths. Models also do not tell you the long-term emotional linkage that you may be building with a consumer. So while they are a valuable part of the measurement arsenal, models should not be taken as the full gospel when making marketing and advertising decisions.

Advertising Measurement

Somewhere along the way, the client will ask the question, "Is this advertising effective?" or more bluntly, "Is this stuff working?" Within the advertising agency, this is always a rather pregnant moment that can lead to a lot of finger pointing, particularly if the client's business is not going well.

Basically, any advertising campaign or specific execution must do the following things:

1. It must get noticed by your target market; it should be seen and remembered.
2. Your target market must know they are being "spoken to"; this is a process or result called "brand linkage."
3. The message must be compelling enough to motivate the target market and group to take the action you want them to take.

We have discussed tracking studies, which get at the question of "Is the advertising working?" From a tracking study, you can determine whether there were changes in your success measures as a result of your campaign. This study should also tell you whether consumers are seeing and remembering your advertising. A tracking study can also help you understand brand linkage of the campaign and it should give you some sense of consumers' motivations. Although tracking studies can give you some good diagnostics about the marketing effort, they give you feedback after the fact. Most advertisers want some assurance they are doing the right thing before they begin investing money in a campaign. Advertisers also want to know how the elements of advertising are going to play out in the campaign.

An advertising campaign is a three-legged stool. The first leg is the message. Your message must be compelling and believable to be effective; this is largely the advertising copy strategy. The second leg is the way the message is conveyed; this is the creative execution. To be effective, it must be memorable and also believable. The third leg of the stool is the media pressure; there must be enough media weight behind the message for the message to register with consumers.

If any one of these three elements of the advertising is not working properly, then you will have a weak advertising campaign. It is about as simple as that. However, breaking apart the advertising process is not as easy as this clinical exercise. Advertising is much more about the whole than the sum of its parts. When Nike was in the beginning stages of building its iconic brand, it used outdoor billboards strategically positioned next to local stadiums, featuring their athletes with little or no brand mention on the board except for the now-famous Nike swoosh logo. This was a wildly successful campaign—helping catapult Nike into the consciousness of almost every athlete or "would-be" athlete on the planet.

However, if you broke this advertising campaign apart, it might never have seen the light of day. There was virtually no "selling proposition" message in the campaign. There was very little "traditional media weight" behind the "nonmessage." Plus, the brand's name often was not even in the ad at all. If you were dissecting this process like a science experiment, you would quickly conclude this campaign would be the greatest loser in history, but although it violated just about every rule known to advertising, it was wildly successful.

This is why advertising professionals can be very quick to loath advertising testing. As an advertising account planner, you are the one party who must bridge the gap between providing meaningful metrics to the client and not letting research get in the way of a potentially great advertising idea. Hey, you knew this was a dangerous job when you took it!

Rational Versus Emotional Message

One way to begin the dialogue on how to test the message and the subsequent creative execution is to look at the type of message that you will be

Table 10.2

Message Emphasis

Rational									Emotional
1	2	3	4	5	6	7	8	9	10
Sales messages			Functional benefits			Emotional benefits as result of functional benefits			Pure emotional benefit

communicating. For example, if you are communicating that you have a one-day sale, that is very different from communicating that by drinking this brand of beer a man will get the woman of his dreams. The more rational the communication, the easier it is to test whether the consumer understands it. The more emotional the message, the tougher it is to ferret out whether the consumer not only understands it but will be moved to think or act in the manner you desire.

One way to start the process is with a simple message-emphasis grid (see Table 10.2). Evaluate the message along the grid from rational to emotional. By working with the client on this simple exercise, you can help come to grips with the type of communication you are crafting, which will help direct the appropriate research to determine its effectiveness.

To the far left side are the most rational messages; examples would be sales messages or limited-time offers. This might be the "one-day sale" mentioned before, or a "50% off" sale. The rational side of the scale isn't exclusive to sales messages. It might be to announce a new company or brand name, to tell consumers that a store has moved, or to announce that a product is now available. There is a lot of advertising that is very rational—and should be, because of the nature of the message—and other advertising that is highly emotional.

The next step up the grid is to discuss a functional benefit. This might be news that Hershey's made its candy bar 50 percent bigger, or it might be that Tide just added a new cleaning agent to its detergent. It could be that a bank has "packaged" its loans in a unique manner. Again, there is nothing to apologize for in delivering a strong functional-benefit message. It has been the foundation for businesses and brands for years.

Before we move on to the emotional side of the scale, we do need to clarify that just because your message is rational does not mean that your advertising has to be blasé or lacking in emotion. The purpose of this exercise is not to say that rational points are not interesting or needed. Some of the best advertising can come out of a rational message. The purpose of this grid is to come to grips with how we might test a message and the creative execution.

As we move onto the emotional side of the grid, we also use the emotional side of a functional benefit. So in the case of Hershey's, a bigger candy bar can lead to a greater "chocolate indulgence." This is the effect of the effect. Some advertisers start with the functional benefit and then move to the emotional side of that benefit when the functional benefit is unique. If it isn't, then you may want to start at the emotional side of the equation.

The final stage of the grid is a pure emotional benefit. Most cosmetics, liquors, and entertainment products are there purely to satisfy some emotional need. As a result, the way you understand this, compared against a one-day sale, requires different methods of testing.

Copytesting

"Copytesting" is a term covering a broad range of advertising research techniques. For some companies and agencies, copytesting is precreative (i.e., before the final form of the message), where consumers are exposed to less-than-finished work to determine how to tweak the final creative product. For others, copytesting is actually testing the finished advertisements, or some stage close to the finished advertisements, to determine how they might stack up against other tested advertising.

Some companies only believe in qualitative testing. Others prefer quantitative testing. There is a dizzying array of research companies and methodologies available to test advertising. Each has its pros and cons. As the advertising account planner, you should challenge the agency and the client to answer some fundamental questions before embarking upon copytesting.

1. What do we expect this advertisement to do?
2. What is our view of how advertising works?
3. What will we do with the outcome of the research?

Once you agree on these issues, you can decide which research method is most appropriate for testing creative. Let's take a look at these questions; then we will discuss various research methods.

The first question, what we expect the advertisement to do, is a basic issue. Do we expect this advertisement to make a sale? Or is it to change an attitude? Perhaps it is to convert a nonuser to a user of a product, or to switch a customer from one brand to another. These are all valid outcomes, but the choice will impact your decision on how to research the advertising.

The second question, of how advertising works, is not a trick question. Many research companies have specific methods designed in a specific manner. If you believe in that manner, then the test will be appropriate for the brand. If you feel otherwise, then you should raise a red flag, stopping the process or at least getting answers to some concerns.

Finally, the question of what you do with the research outcome is crucial. Is the outcome designed to just give diagnostics of the advertisement so you can see how it "performs," or is it designed to give feedback to the creative group to enhance the advertising? Then there is the dreaded question of what happens if the advertisements test poorly. Do you scrap the campaign and start over, or is there something that you can change to make it effective? All of these issues, even though they may be ticklish, should be discussed beforehand, rather than in the middle of the research and creative processes.

Once you agree on these questions, you are off and running to determine whether you should test or not and, if so, what would be the appropriate method to use.

Qualitative Testing

Qualitative research is very important in the advertising creation process. If you want to get spontaneous, rich, and undirected feedback to a proposed advertisement, qualitative research is a must. It is the truest way to get at the emotional underpinnings of what the advertisement conveys.

Let's face it: you are not likely to fill out a questionnaire saying that an advertisement moved you or that you felt any emotions from reading a piece of advertising copy. Consumers are emotional beings, but are even more so rational beings. Observing how consumers react to advertising is a very good barometer of how it will work in the marketplace.

Qualitative research starts with a trained moderator, who works either with a single consumer or with a small group of consumers to help bring out their feelings and attitudes toward various stimuli. Many times, trained moderators use projective techniques, helping consumers articulate their feelings toward a brand and an advertisement.

Perhaps the best qualitative research information is conducted using one-on-one in-depth interviews, where the moderator and the consumer engage in a deep and probing understanding of the feelings about or created by the advertising. Typically, these interviews are thirty minutes to an hour in length, with the consumer asked to view whole series of advertising.

Many advertisers use focus groups as the "standard bearer" for testing creative concepts. Focus groups consist of a trained moderator and eight to twelve consumers of similar characteristics, in a room where the advertiser and agency can view the participants from behind a one-way mirror. The popularity of focus groups is that, in an hour or two, the advertisers can see reactions from a "representative" sample of their customers. Focus groups usually have quite a bit of interplay between respondents. While this can yield some rich results, it can more often than not lead to going in the direction of whoever is the strongest respondent. Respondent bias can come into play very quickly with focus groups, even with a seasoned moderator.

A compromise position lies in triads. This is where there are three consumers in the room with a moderator. The goal here is to gain the more in-depth and probing nature of one-on-one approach yet with a small amount of group-dynamic interaction.

The upside of qualitative research is that you will get a good feel for the kind of emotional response your advertising message will deliver. You should also get a good feel for the clarity of the communication and whether it is compelling. However, all of these are a "feel." They are not "hard" data (firm and projectable research findings) in the truest sense.

The downside to any qualitative research is that you cannot provide the specific numerical data that many CEOs prefer to use to make decisions. It cannot give you the specifics of the communication or a breakdown of various diagnostics. From a communication perspective, you really cannot tell whether the advertisement or execution will break through the clutter in the given environment. The advertising's ability to be recalled or remembered is information qualitative research cannot provide.

To make qualitative research more statistically projectable, some research companies have gone to great lengths to add sophisticated components to their measures. Some have employed galvanic skin response, pupil dilation, eye movement, voice stress, facial-expression coding, and even brain-wave monitoring. There are research companies using a mixture of these components, most often along with traditional moderator-led projection techniques, to add a layer of statistical validation to the qualitative measurement.

In the end, as with all research, the goal is to aid in your judgment of what works and what does not, and not to replace that judgment. For those who are very risk averse and want support for their decisions, there is a bevy of quantitative research companies that do copytesting.

Quantitative Research

There are a number of companies who use quantitative research methods to provide a diagnostic of advertising effectiveness. This research is primarily television execution-based and is also largely driven by the packaged-goods industry.

This type of research typically tests television commercials in an animatic form. An animatic is not a finished commercial but is highly representative of the finished advertisement. Usually the goal of quantitative testing is to determine which of several commercials should go into production. The power of much quantitative testing lies in its ability to predict, based on the test, the future sales potential of the commercial. Over the years, the research companies using this type of testing have collected in-market validation of their research methodologies.

Before we get into the different specific methods, it is important to understand the dividing line for most researchers about how advertising works. The advertising research community is largely divided into two "camps"; the first camp is recall-based and the second camp is persuasion-based.

Since the early days of television, the first widely used pretesting measure for this medium was Burke's Day-After Recall Score, which measured advertising effectiveness based on the ability of the advertising creative execution to leave a specific memory with consumers. This method used some exposure to an advertisement, typically in a television program shown on one day, and the next day consumers were asked to recall advertisements that they had seen in this program.

Recall is based on the simple principle that advertising that gets remembered works better than advertising that isn't remembered. However, during the 1970s, Procter & Gamble concluded that recall of commercials did not necessarily correlate with sales. Although subsequent research has shown that recall does indeed correlate with sales, the Procter & Gamble study rocked the advertising research world.

In the 1970s, pretesting research shifted gears to focus on persuasion. Persuasion is the measure of getting someone to purchase the brand. This view of advertising is that the message should be able to be converted into short-term sales and that this conversion can be predicted within the marketplace. This degree of conversion is measured by taking a split sample (control and test groups), with one group shown your commercial and the other not shown the commercial, and then to measure the difference in purchase intent between the two samples. This can be done on a pre- and postbasis or just by contrasting the two samples.

Figure 10.3   **Copy Effect Index Correlated with Sales Impact**

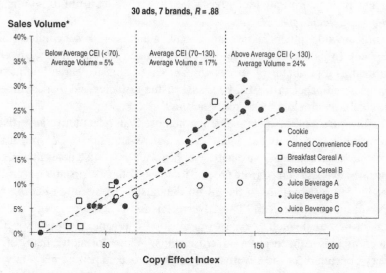

30 ads, 7 brands, *R* = .88

Sales Volume*

Below Average CEI (< 70). Average Volume = 5%

Average CEI (70–130). Average Volume = 17%

Above Average CEI (> 130). Average Volume = 24%

- Cookie
- Canned Convenience Food
- Breakfast Cereal A
- Breakfast Cereal B
- Juice Beverage A
- Juice Beverage B
- Juice Beverage C

Copy Effect Index

*Incremental sales volume contribution per 100 incremental GRPs, as % of brand's average weekly sales volume.

Source: Ipsos-ASI 2005.

Many large packaged-goods companies use this approach and build large databases of research on their commercials so they can see how one commercial stacks up against a historical view of commercials. Some of the larger packaged-goods manufacturers have their own databases of commercials and results so they can do their own prognosticating about the possible success of a future advertising endeavor.

One of the leading advertising research companies, Ipsos-ASI, has developed a copy-effect score, combining recall and persuasion into a single number, indicating the net commercial effect. Their copy-effect index (CEI) score is then used as a barometer of success for the television creative execution. Figure 10.3 is an example of how the CEI correlated with sales impact for some packaged-goods categories studied by Ipsos-ASI.

As you can see from this example, the CEI serves as a strong indicator of a commercial's short-term or incremental-volume effects on a brand. Those commercials having less than a 70 CEI do not generate much incremental volume, but those with a CEI higher than 130 generate a lot of incremental volume. In the packaged-goods arena, studies such as this are the gold standard for how commercials get on the air. In today's short-term accountability climate, this research is very appealing to brand management and corporate executives who must make multimillion-dollar advertising decisions.

Meanwhile, others argue that how much a person likes a commercial is the key to its success. Likeability of a commercial was empirically confirmed as a predictor of success by an Advertising Research Foundation project and paper in 1991. Many advertising agencies and marketers look to likability as a key measure for success.

Regardless of the quantitative method used, all quantitative advertising research methods rely on the use of normative data; this is the comparison of your advertisement to a database of historical advertisements that is, to a norm or average gained from previous studies. Your advertisement is graded or judged by comparison, based on diagnostics of attention getting and persuasion compared to "like advertisements." This normative database might be broad, such as data from all food companies, or very specific, such as only canned pasta advertisements. While normative data can be very appealing for the advertiser to see how its commercial may stack up compared to past efforts, it can be easily misleading. No two advertising commercials are designed for the same purpose for the same target market. In these situations, it is important to understand clearly the methodology, to ensure the test is weighted properly, and that normative data are meaningful to the process when used.

Even though advertising research has given us much richer diagnostics than in the past, in the end, judgments still need to be made. One cannot abdicate responsibility for the advertising by merely seeing whether the advertisement reached a certain copytesting metric. Research can certainly help improve advertising and it can reduce some risks associated with it, helping those ultimately responsible for its success to make important decisions, but it is no substitute for common sense and experience.

So, where does all this leave us? Do not despair. There are a lot of smart researchers out there who tout their methods as the "be all and end all." There are research methods for all occasions and situations. The issue you face as the advertising account planner is to ensure that the advertising will work, without taking the soul out of the actual advertisement. You walk a fine line between the client, who is seeking reassurance that his investment will pay off, and the creative group that is shooting for the next big idea. Your role is to make sure that any advertising research helps improve the creative product while reassuring the client that this is the right campaign

Table 10.3

Typical Advertising Effect Research

Type of advertising effect		Typical research
Sales	➡	Company database and records
Consumer buying behavior	➡	Retail scanning data and/or customer research
Consumer purchase intent	➡	Primary quantitative research (AA&U)
Attitudes toward brand	➡	Primary quantitative tracking research
Awareness of the brand	➡	Primary quantitative tracking research
Attitudes of advertising	➡	Primary quantitative tracking research for market changes and qualitative research for executions
Recall of advertising	➡	Primary quantitative tracking research
Exposure to advertising	➡	Syndicated media research

for the brand. It is not always an easy task but, by working through the issues, you can make it a fair and beneficial process.

Advertising Effects and Research Methods

We have discussed a wide range of issues and success criteria for advertising and marketing campaigns. From a pure advertising-effect perspective, while there are many research methods to arrive at a measure of success, the types of research are fairly standard. To aid your understanding, look at the recap of the types of advertising effects and the typical research methods employed to understand them (see Table 10.3).

As you move through the course of measuring advertising's impact on a company, product, or brand, keep in mind that there are short-term and long-term effects of advertising. The short-term impacts are captured with sales and purchase-behavior information. The long-term aspects are captured in attitudinal studies. The diagnostics of advertising copy and media pressure can be captured via a combination of research types as well.

In conclusion, it is important to remember that advertising works in many different ways. It is important to help your client define success from two essential perspectives of the advertising objectives: a marketing outcome and a communication outcome. The role of the advertising account planner in this process is to keep the objectives at the forefront of your thoughts and to guide the client to the proper methods of defining success. Ultimately, the advertising client's success will be the advertising agency's success. No matter how success is quantified, it usually boils down to trust between these two parties.

Review Questions

1. What is equity? What is brand equity?
2. What is awareness? Attitude? Usage? How do they differ? How are they alike?
3. What is tracking? What is building equity? How do they differ? How are they alike?
4. How are all these factors reflected in consumers' behavior?

Discussion Questions

1. How can awareness, attitude, and usage be matched up to create an analysis of advertising success?
2. How can building equity and tracking be matched up to create an analysis of advertising success?
3. What is the real measure of advertising success? Why don't advertisers use that in their measurements of advertising success?
4. What do we use instead (surrogates)?

Exercises

1. Analyze the advertising campaigns for two (or more) competing brands. Which do you believe is more successful? Why?
2. Now try to find sales and/or profit figures for these brands. Compare these figures with your analyses of their campaigns.

CBC Case Study

Use the CBC case information from Chapter 1.

1. Plan success measures for your potential advertising campaign for CBC.
2. Now plan your research techniques to measure this success.
3. Compare these success measures with your SWOT analysis (see Chapter 2).

Additional Sources

Gregory, James R. *The Best of Branding: Best Practices in Corporate Branding.* New York: McGraw-Hill, 2003.

Kelley, Larry D., and Donald W. Jugenheimer. *Advertising Media Planning: A Brand Management Approach.* Armonk, NY: M.E. Sharpe, 2004.

Lonier, Terri. *Smart Strategies for Growing Your Business.* New York: Wiley, 1999.

Miller, Jon, and David Muir. *The Business of Brands.* New York: Wiley, 2004.

Sullivan, Luke. *Hey, Whipple, Squeeze This: A Guide to Creating Great Ads.* New York: Wiley, 2003.

Chapter 11

Business-to-Business Case Study: Recon Software

Recon Software is the brainchild of two graduate students at the University of California at Berkeley. Their initial work involved optimizing production systems through the use of neural network software. However, they discovered that they could apply this same tool to build an ever-upgraded firewall providing a defense against computer viruses. They quickly patented the neural network software and named it Recon. The name is short for reconnaissance.

Recon software gained strength as the product gained server mass. Because it was a constantly learning program, the more servers and defense it had access to, the greater its ability to learn which viruses were possible. This information fed into the software's ability to upgrade itself continually and to block not only existing viruses but also predict and adapt to future viruses as well.

The students' professor introduced them to a Silicon Valley venture-capital firm that provided the seed money to develop the software and take it to market. The two students formed their company and promptly enlisted the help of an advertising agency to market the product. The venture-capital company had given Recon only a six-month timeframe in which to launch their product before the bank "pulled" its funding. So, making the right decision in terms of positioning and marketing was crucial for the young entrepreneurs.

Software Marketplace

The software marketplace was huge (see Figure 11.1 and Table 11.1). The defense segment into which the two students stumbled was nearly a $10 billion worldwide market. The major players in this market were IBM, which dominated computer mainframe protection, as well as other aggressive companies, including Oracle, Computer Associates, and niche companies such as BMC Software. All of these companies had products in the defense arena, with the

Table 11.1

Worldwide Security Software Market Forecast by Channels: 2005 to 2008
($ millions)

Channels	Year 2005	2006	2007	2008	Compound annual growth (%) (2005–8)
Direct	5,357	6,065	6,082	7,510	11.9
Multitier distribution	2,513	2,844	3,189	3,520	11.9
OEM	1,047	1,166	1,286	1,395	10.1
Single-tier resale	3,033	3,618	4,269	4,950	17.7
Total	11,950	13,694	15,546	17,375	13.3

Figure 11.1   **Worldwide Total Network Security Revenue**

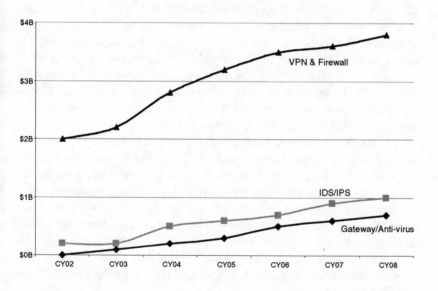

latter three being more servers-based and IBM being more mainframe-based.

The companies that could benefit most from Recon's software were very large companies having complex computer systems. The venture-capital team helped the students identify the target markets and groups. The more complex systems included pulp and paper mills, auto manufacturing plants, oil refineries, electric and gas utilities, and local, state, and national governments, as shown in Table 11.2.

Table 11.2

Systems Software Market

Category	Headquarter companies (number)	Total software revenue ($ billions)
Pulp and paper mills	10	5.2
Auto manufacturing	20	7.9
Oil refineries	30	7.4
Gas/electric utilities	300	12.3
Government (city, state, and federal)	7,000	45.2
Total	7,495	78.0

All of these companies would benefit from Recon's software because they could link all their plants to the same defense software programs that could learn from one another to maximize their virus protection. However, all of these companies were well established with their systems and the students wondered whether the companies would be likely to try something new. The "going-in" or entry cost for Recon was not inexpensive. The cost was $500,000 to set up the system plus a minimum monthly fee of $10,000 that escalated depending upon the server volume of the company. On the other hand, if a plant had a business interruption of one day, it could cost the company well over $1 million dollars. In other cases, an outage of any type would have dire consequences (see Table 11.3).

To complicate things more, the students learned that there were multiple layers to selling such a business product. There were IT managers who had to be consulted on any software purchase. IT personnel were responsible for maintaining and installing the product. There were operations managers who depended upon the software to help them with their jobs. There were financial managers who reviewed all purchases and there were senior managers who had to give the final blessing. This was nothing compared to selling to the government. The pair learned that they must first apply to be a government contractor and then go through a bid process before being considered.

To help the students get through this process, a veteran software marketer developed a risk/reward matrix to help them understand the decision process and how each position would react to the new software (see Figure 11.2). He also hired some young and aggressive sales people who could go anywhere to make the sale.

The students were very excited about their software and thought Recon was a "cool" name. Their first reaction was to position this as a hip new

Table 11.3

Cost of Business Interruption

Category	Dollars per day per single plant ($ millions)
Pulp and paper mills	0.7
Auto manufacturing	1.2
Oil refineries	3.0
Gas/electric utilities	2.2
Government (city, state, and federal)	1.5

Figure 11.2   **Risk/Reward Matrix**

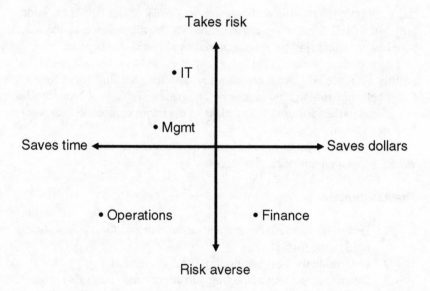

product. Yet they were concerned that if they appeared to be too irreverent, they would not be taken seriously.

This information constituted the briefing that the account planner was given for Recon Software. The account planner knew it was largely up to him to help bring some clarity to this situation for Recon. The students were too inexperienced in marketing and the venture team had provided working capital but not much else. This project would involve market analy-

Table 11.4

Target Profile

Occupation	Typical demographics	Occupational mindset
IT	Male, age 35–45, college graduate	Looks for latest technology to make a difference
Operations	Male, age 35–45, some college	Looks to keep things running smoothly and quickly
Finance	Male, age 45–60, MBA	Looks to control costs and save money where possible
Management	Male, age 45–65, college/MBA	Looking for competitive edge

sis, positioning, and ultimately some sort of marketing communications program to sell this software. And time was of the essence as the sales people were clamoring for sales materials and marketing support.

The account planner quickly looked for any information he could find on this audience. He came across a few articles shedding some light on buyer behavior for large purchases by companies. Table 11.4 brought a bit of a "face" to the various target markets of the major companies that would be potential software buyers.

There was not a lot of time to lose. The account planner had only a few weeks to put a plan together for Recon.

The Assignment

1. Determine the best segment and target(s) to gain the quickest stronghold in the market.
2. Determine the best positioning for that segment.
3. Determine the best marketing and advertising strategy to promote Recon to that segment.
4. Translate the strategy into a creative brief.
5. Determine what research is needed for the brand while doing the initial plan.
6. Provide a point of view on positioning the Recon brand in short-term versus long-term contexts.

Chapter 12
Packaged-Goods Case Study: Chiffon Margarine

Pinnacle Foods is an aggregator of venerable old brands that are in need of restaging. One of the recently acquired brands in its stable of products was Chiffon margarine. Chiffon had great success in the 1970s and 1980s as one of the brand leaders when butter surrendered to margarine as the spread of choice. During this time, Chiffon had some award-winning advertising with "Mother Nature" as the spokesperson for the brand. In the television commercial executions, "Mother Nature" would proclaim Chiffon to be so fresh and natural that "It isn't nice to fool Mother Nature."

Since the 1980s, the Chiffon brand has been bought and sold more than once. It became largely a trade-supported brand with no advertising or marketing for the past ten years. However, the new brand manager on Chiffon at Pinnacle Foods felt that the brand had some "upside" potential. The firm had come up with a breakthrough way of enhancing the brand with natural flavors. Based on significant product testing, Pinnacle was ready to "roll out" sweet and unsweetened versions of the margarine as well as margarine with cinnamon flavoring. The brand manager felt that he could do with margarine what had been done in other food categories such as mustard, ketchup, and other condiments, that is, create some excitement and new usage opportunities. He also felt that he could take some market share away from the cooking sprays and oils that had flavorings but were inconsistent in their usage.

As he analyzed the product benefits, he realized that foods with natural flavoring are appealing to consumers. A homemaker could basically enhance any meal without changing the way it was prepared. In today's fast-paced world, he felt that benefit would be very appealing. The flavorings were also all natural, which kept with the natural tradition of the brand, and he felt this was a big plus as well. In taste tests, the margarine fared very well, with consumers saying the cinnamon flavor really enhanced their foods. Others talked about how they liked the sweeter margarine. Consumers said that this characteristic made up for not using sugar

Table 12.1

Chiffon Case: Margarine Category

Total category sales: $861.5 million

Brand	Share (%)	Advertising used
Private label	23.5	None
I Can't Believe It's Not Butter	12.7	TV, print
Shedd's County Crock	11.6	TV, print
Blue Bonnet	10.9	FSI
Parkay	8.5	TV, FSI
Imperial	8.5	None
Land O'Lakes	5.5	TV
Fleishmann's	4.0	Print
Chiffon	2.0	None
Other brands (local/regional)	12.8	—
Total	100.0	

or other sweeteners in their cooking. This final focus group got the brand manager thinking there might even be a nutritional angle that he could exploit in the brand's advertising.

The margarine category represents $861.5 million of revenue, with a host of brands competing for market share. There was quite a bit of competition for this market, with the majority of brands spending many dollars on marketing. The marketing medium of choice for the category was television. Many of the brands also used women's magazines as an advertising medium and many also used coupons distributed in FSIs. Table 12.1 summarizes the competition and the market share.

As the brand manager reviewed the category, what made him concerned was the large private-label percentage of sales. This fact signaled to him that the category had deteriorated into a general commodity. He wanted the new flavors of Chiffon to command a premium price, but he feared the category might not be able to support a more premium-priced entry. He was also concerned Chiffon had become a "price brand," competing and sold on low price, because it had long since quit advertising. It would be a tough road to command a premium price for Chiffon given its low market share and history of not promoting the brand with marketing support.

The advertising agency had just completed an assignment on defining the demographics of the category (see Table 12.2). The category consumer was a 25–54-year-old homemaker, with two children. The fre-

Table 12.2

Margarine Category: Frequent User

Demographics	Users (%)	Index
Females	75	150
18–24	9	80
25–34	17	100
35–44	21	105
45–54	22	110
55–64	16	108
65+	15	90
Graduate college +	20	80
Any college	24	60
High school graduate	36	107
Not high school graduate	20	133
Employed fulltime	60	115
Married	65	112
1 child at home	18	105
2–3 children at home	22	125
4+ children at home	15	132

quent buyers of margarine were not highly educated, which concerned the brand manager as he considered how he might position the product. A debate raged in the company about whom he should target. Should it be the current category user, or should he stake out some ground with consumers who were very much in tune with the brand regardless of how much margarine they used?

To shed more light on the margarine consumer, the advertising agency also profiled the margarine consumer's buying lifestyles. Table 12.3 illustrates the key buying lifestyles that the agency found of interest.

After reviewing the buying lifestyles, the brand manager became very concerned about what to think. He saw that the consumers indicated that they would not pay for quality, yet they made impulsive purchases. Could he get them to take a chance and try his brand?

The advertising agency also delved into some consumer-trend information on food trends and found that there were a few key trends that were very applicable to this situation, as shown in Table 12.4.

As the brand manager reviewed the latter trends, he was becoming even more confused. He saw the trends were in his favor, but which one should he focus on?

Table 12.3

Chiffon Case: Margarine Consumer Buying Styles

Attitude	Index
Enjoy spending time with my family	130
I like to do unconventional things	95
Important to be attractive	120
Worth paying extra for quality	85
Decide what I want before shopping	75
I am easily swayed by others	110
I am the first to try new things	100
I buy items on impulse	140

Source: Simmons Market Research Bureau 2004.

Table 12.4

Top Ten Consumer Food Values

Value	Referred (%)
Deliciousness	41
Convenience	21
Wellness	20
Experience	14
Fun	13
Quality	12
Simplicity	12
Balance	12
Authenticity	11
Control	10

Source: Iconoculture 2004. Reprinted with permission.

The agency also came across some research discussing the body types of various consumers (see Table 12.5). The researchers looked at the frequent margarine buyers but also looked at consumers who liked spicy foods as an indicator of consumers who might try new items. The results of the study showed there were marked differences between the two groups.

Now the brand manager's head was spinning. He called a brand summit meeting with the advertising agency team to discuss all the research and the brand. He said that the agency needed to sift through the data and give him a recommendation on how to proceed with supporting the brand. The

Table 12.5

Chiffon Case: Waist Brand Study

Type	Frequent margarine user	Spicy food eater
Underweight	62	110
Normal	91	120
Overweight	115	105
Obese	135	75

Source: Source: Simmons Market Research Bureau 2004.

agency president turned to the account planner and gave him the following assignment.

Assignment

1. Determine the appropriate brand position for Chiffon and based on that positioning develop a creative brief for the agency.
2. Before determining the positioning, we need to develop a recommendation on the best target market to tackle with this brand.
3. Because Chiffon had some advertising that was quite good in its day, perhaps we should review it and consider writing a story about it and the brand.
4. While we don't have much media information to go on, we should get the media team prepared to help launch this brand. How should we go about doing so?

Chapter 13

Retail Case Study: Kmart and Sears

It is not every day an that account planner sits in the office of the chairman of one of the largest retail holding companies in the world, but pretend that there you are, sitting by the desk of the man who just orchestrated the merger of Kmart and Sears to form Sears Holding Company.

He has asked for you to come to his office because he has an enormous task ahead of him. Now that he owns both Kmart and Sears, what should he do with them? Should he combine them into one brand? And if so, which brand should he choose? Or should he keep them as two separate brands and try to outflank Wal-Mart and Target, the key competitors in the discount retailing arena?

As the chairman mulled over these decisions, he called you into his office because he wanted to get a consumer perspective on this decision without any emotional bias. Obviously, the marketing directors of each company, Sears and Kmart, have reasons for wanting to maintain control over their marketing decisions. Because he knows you are with the advertising agency that is going to support the brand regardless of its outcome, he has called you into the office to gain your perspective on this move.

He first explains why he merged Kmart with Sears. He felt that size and scope were the only way to compete in the retailing world dominated by Wal-Mart. Table 13.1 demonstrates that very point. However, even the combined Kmart and Sears entity was only a quarter the size of Wal-Mart.

The chairman goes on to say he feels that there would be operational efficiencies in buying merchandise and having central warehouses for both chains. He sees there is potential to sell some of Sears' brand merchandise, particularly Kenmore appliances and Craftsman tools, in Kmart. Plus, he sees potential to sell some of Kmart's fashion brands, such as Martha Stewart, Route 66, and Jaclyn Smith, in Sears stores. But he feels that both Sears and Kmart are not great overall brands. To him, Sears seems dated while Kmart is still known as the "blue light special" place.

Although both Sears and Kmart have fashion brands (see Table 13.2), neither has made much progress in cracking the discount fashion business, which is now dominated by Target. Even Wal-Mart is having a tough time

Table 13.1

Top Retail Sales Leaders

Company	Revenue
Wal-Mart	174.2
Sears	23.2
Target	41.3
Kmart	23.0
Federated Stores	17.7
May Co.	15.0
	14.0

Source: 2005 Retail Business Market Research Handbook.

Table 13.2

Key Brands Owned by Each Retailer

Sears	Kmart
Land's End	Martha Stewart
Craftsman Tools	Jaclyn Smith
Kenmore Appliances	Joe Boxer
Whirlpool	Route 66
Frigidaire	Sesame Street

catching Target in this important facet of merchandising. It is one of the key areas that consistently brings customers to the store. This concerns the chairman considerably. He needs to make the right move with the brands and he needs to build a retailer of the future. The chairman asks you to come back in two weeks with a recommendation on how you see the business from a consumer perspective and how this view might determine the marketing and advertising approach for the company.

The next day, the president of the advertising agency sits with you and your planning team to discuss the situation. In the course of the discussion, the planning team has begun to assemble various pieces of research that might be helpful in figuring out the two brands.

One interesting piece of research that the planning team has come across is a cross-shopping matrix showing the percentage of shoppers who shop at various retailers and a loyalty factor for each (see Table 13.3). The team also had asked the media team to develop a demographic profile of Kmart and Sears consumers. Table 13.4 is the profile of each customer base. The

Table 13.3

Cross Shopping of Consumers Regarding Mass Merchandising

Company	Sears consumers who shop at (%)	Kmart consumers who shop at (%)	Consumers who shop predominantly at (%)
Sears	100	35	20
Kmart	20	100	10
Wal-Mart	85	90	50
Target	60	70	40

Table 13.4

Demographic Profile of Sears and Kmart Shopper

Demographic	Sears		Kmart	
	%	Index	%	Index
Male	45	94	36	75
Female	55	106	64	123
18–24	4	34	9	79
25–34	13	78	17	99
35–44	18	94	21	105
45–54	26	131	22	110
55–64	19	128	16	108
65+	20	115	15	90
Median HHI	$63,000		$52,000	
Married	74	127	58	90
Not Married	36	85	42	110
White	84	108	77	99
African American	9	90	12	120
Hispanic	7	65	11	135

Source: Mediamark Research, Inc. 2004. Reprinted with permission.

team has also identified consumer buying styles that the two brands have in common and those that are unique to each (see Table 13.5).

After reviewing this information, the president asks whether you feel that you could make an agency recommendation from it. She is concerned it isn't enough information from which to draw the proper insights that could ultimately lead to making important decisions. The president of the agency says that she would be willing to fund primary research to under-

Table 13.5

Buying Styles of Mass Merchandiser Consumers

Buying Statement	Kmart	Sears	Target	Wal-Mart
I am an impulsive shopper	116	95	125	105
I am willing to pay more for quality	105	125	120	90
I enjoy owning good things	130	110	140	105
I am always looking for new ideas	115	90	135	115
I like a simple life	80	140	85	110
I am good at fixing things	100	150	95	120
I decide what I want before shopping	90	125	80	120
I am optimistic	115	105	120	105
I find that I am swayed easily by others	120	90	130	105
I try not to worry about the future	115	105	120	105

Source: Simmons Market Research Bureau 2004.

stand the situation better, but given the time constraints, what could the agency do that would be meaningful?

While the assignment seems clear, the president of the agency decides to write up the assignment just to ensure that everyone has the proper focus on what to accomplish.

Assignment

1. Develop a SWOT analysis to understand better where the opportunities are for the two brands.
2. Develop a positioning exercise for each brand and determine where you might position each separately.
3. From this positioning exercise, determine whether one brand is clearly superior to another.
4. Develop a creative brief for the brand or brands that survive the positioning exercise.
5. Develop a research plan to help map out a process for success and how to track progress toward it.

Index

About the Authors

Larry D. Kelley is an executive vice president with FogartyKleinMonroe, where he is responsible for the strategic planning arm of the agency called the Targeting Group. The Targeting Group pulls together media, research, and account planning into a single insight entity for this $250 million, Texas-based agency. Kelley oversees strategic planning on all agency clients, including ConAgra Foods, Kroger, Riviana Foods, Daisy Sour Cream, Conoco retail, Mission Foods, Waste Management, and Advance Auto Parts.

Prior to joining FogartyKleinMonroe, Kelley served in senior media and media research management positions in BBD&O, Bozell & Jacobs, and Bloom Agency. His work has spanned a wide variety of accounts from American Airlines to Quaker Oats to Bell South.

Kelley's consumer behavior insights have earned him recognition as an industry leader, including four EFFIES awards for advertising effectiveness. He is also widely quoted in trade publications such as *Adweek, Advertising Age,* and the *Journal of Advertising.*

Kelley holds a B.S. in journalism from the University of Kansas and an M.A. in marketing communication from the University of Texas at Austin.

Donald W. Jugenheimer is professor of advertising at Texas Tech University. His teaching specialties are media management, media economics, and advertising media.

Since earning his Ph.D. in communications from the University of Illinois with a specialization in advertising and a minor in marketing, Dr. Jugenheimer has been a tenured member of the faculties at the University of Kansas, Louisiana State University (where he became the first person to hold the Manship Distinguished Professorship in Journalism), Fairleigh Dickinson University, and Southern Illinois University.

Jugenheimer has written or co-written twelve books and many articles and papers. He has spoken before a variety of academic and professional organizations, and has served as president of the American Academy of Advertising and as advertising division head of the Association for Education in Journalism and Mass Communication. He also was business manager for the founding of the *Journal of Advertising*. He has lectured and conducted workshops in several countries and is on the guest faculty of the Executive Media MBA program for the Turku School of Economics and Business Administration in Finland.

As a consultant, Jugenheimer has worked with such firms as American Airlines, IBM, Century 21 Real Estate, Aetna Insurance, Pacific Telesis, and the U.S. Army Recruiting Command. He has also conducted research for a variety of enterprises, including the U.S. Department of Health, Education and Welfare, the International Association of Business Communicators, and National Liberty Life Insurance.